GOOD NEWS

Good News

The Advent of Salvation in the Gospel of Luke

Darrin W. Snyder Belousek

LITURGICAL PRESS
Collegeville, Minnesota

www.litpress.org

Cover design by Stefan Killen Design. Cover art © ThinkStock.

1 2 3 4 5 6 7 8 9

Library of Congress Cataloging-in-Publication Data

Belousek, Darrin W. Snyder, 1969–
Good news : the advent of salvation in the gospel of Luke / Darrin W. Snyder Belousek.
pages cm
Includes bibliographical references.
ISBN 978-0-8146-3758-6 — ISBN 978-0-8146-3783-8 (ebook)
1. Bible. Luke—Criticism, interpretation, etc. 2. Salvation—Biblical teaching. I. Title.

BS2595.6.S25B45 2014
234—dc23 2013045670

But the angel said to them,
"Do not be afraid;
for see—I am bringing you
good news of great joy for all the people:
to you is born this day in the city of David
a Savior, who is the Messiah, the Lord."

—Luke 2:10-11

CONTENTS

PREFACE

It is commonly believed among Christians that Jesus is Savior only insofar as he dies on the cross and is raised from the dead. The divine purpose of Jesus' coming is often reduced further, to his death: as the traditional American folk carol tells it, "Jesus the Savior did come for to die" ("I Wonder as I Wander"). Having reduced the saving work of Jesus to his death, Christians then narrow the point of salvation to our life beyond death: Jesus was born to die, and by his death and resurrection we are reborn to life in heaven.

Luke's gospel tells a bigger story of salvation: Jesus is Savior throughout his life, not only in death and resurrection; and the salvation that Jesus brings has good news for us here and now, on earth as well as in heaven. Just before making his final approach to Jerusalem, where he anticipates meeting suffering and death, Jesus is met by a rich ruler, who asks, "Good Teacher, what must I do to inherit eternal life?" (Luke 18:18). When the man declares that he has kept the whole Torah his whole life but then declines to do now as the Teacher instructs—sell his possessions, distribute to the poor, and become a follower—Jesus says, "How hard it is for those who have wealth to enter the kingdom of God!" (v. 24). Those listening wonder, "Then who can be saved?" (v. 26). And Peter, speaking for the disciples, says, "Look, we have left our homes and followed you" (v. 28). What, they ask, is the reward for risking all to follow Jesus? Jesus answers with this good news: "Truly I tell you, there is no one who has left house or wife or brothers or parents or children, for the sake of the kingdom of God, who will not get back very much more in this age, and in the age to come eternal life" (vv. 29-30). The kingdom of God has come near in Jesus; and those who put their faith in Jesus and commit their lives to the kingdom will receive salvation—not only eternal life "in the age to come" but also "very much more" than what they left behind "in this age."

This book explores that larger meaning of salvation—that "very much more"—in Luke's gospel. Through reflections on the stories and songs of the coming of Jesus the Messiah, this book explicates the manifold message of "good news." Each of the seven chapters addresses a different dimension of the good news: the proclamation of good news by the prophet of the Lord; deliverance from fear and striving for those who receive the good news; healing from sin and sickness for those who pursue the good news; repentance and revival for those who respond to the good news; justice in word and deed by those who are convicted and converted by the good news; praise in songs of peace and freedom by those who put their hope in the good news; and mission in service to the nations by those who heed the good news and commit their lives to God's kingdom. As we will see, another hymn better captures the full tenor of Luke's story of the Messiah's advent: "Come, thou long-expected Jesus, born to set thy people free, from our fears and sins release us, let us find our rest in thee" (Charles Wesley).

Fully accessible to laypersons yet substantially informed by biblical scholarship, both keenly aware of spiritual concerns and passionately engaged with social issues, this book could be utilized in various ways. First, because it gives special emphasis to the story and songs of Jesus' birth from Luke's gospel, this book would benefit the general reader seeking the "bigger picture" and "deeper meaning" of Advent and Christmas. Second, insofar as the reflections sound out both spiritual and literal meanings in the biblical message, thoughtfully interrelating text with text and freely imagining "the story within the story," this book would aid pastors and clergy preparing to proclaim the word to a church and world needing to hear "good news." Third, attentive to both personal and social dimensions of the biblical message and its concrete relevance for our contemporary experience, this book would bolster those striving for justice, freedom, and peace in the name of God's kingdom. Fourth, conversant with biblical scholarship and theological perspectives, this book would serve teachers and students as a supplementary text for courses of study in Luke's gospel or biblical theology. Although readers can benefit from the insights of this book at any time of year, some may wish to approach it specifically during Advent and Christmas. If so, chapters 2 through 5 may correspond to the four weeks of Advent, chapter 6 to Christmas, and chapter 7 to Epiphany.

Two streams of Christian tradition converge in this book. The first is my theological formation within the Anabaptist-Mennonite tradition. This tradition emphasizes discipleship as an essential aspect of salvation—being saved by the grace of God and following Jesus in the way of peace are inseparable. The key text of this tradition is the Sermon on the Mount. The second stream of tradition is my spiritual formation by Benedictine prayer, which I have practiced on a daily basis for many years. The Benedictine way also emphasizes discipleship, community, and peace, but its vision and practice are rooted as much in the Psalms as in the gospels.

This book thus brings together the Anabaptist tradition of peace theology and the Benedictine tradition of spiritual practice in an imaginative and challenging way. I seek to re-root peace and justice in the soil of salvation and spirituality, to complement the Anabaptist approach that emphasizes the ethics of discipleship. And I seek to do this by reflecting on the meaning of salvation in the coming of Jesus, especially as implicit in the canticles from Luke's gospel that shape Benedictine practice. This book, then, offers a vision of salvation that is grounded in grace and nurtured by prayer, relevant to both spiritual and social dimensions of life, and inseparable from doing justice and seeking peace.

I write not only out of a tradition of theology and practice of prayer but also out of personal experience in the mission of the church. The major writing of this book (1999–2005) was done while I was on assignment in voluntary service through the Mennonite Church—first as an urban worker in South Bend, Indiana, and then as an international teacher in Lithuania. My mission experience has provided me with tangible evidence that Jesus' promise to his followers is indeed trustworthy—those who leave homes and families for the sake of the kingdom really do receive back "very much more." Finally, I write out of the shared experience of a nation at war. During a decade of "war on terror," I have wondered: What might "good news" of salvation mean to those of us who are situated securely in a nation that is unequaled in economic prosperity and military might and yet is gripped by fear and grasping for dominance? What does it mean for us to hear the message of the prophet that we will have peace when our enemy has peace?

My primary focus in Luke's gospel is on the nativity narrative and the thematic threads that link the story and songs of Jesus' birth to the words and ways of Jesus' ministry and the early church. My method of working with the biblical text and drawing out its meaning is neither "systematic" nor "scholarly," strictly speaking. While I do interpret texts in light of their historical situation where doing so helps amplify either the meaning or force of the text, I do not employ the standard scholarly methods of historical, form, or literary criticism. Concerning the Lukan canticles, for example, biblical scholars are interested in such questions as who actually wrote them or what historical communities produced them, and under what circumstances; whether the author of Luke composed the nativity narrative around them or inserted them later into an already composed narrative; and how they compare to other Jewish poetic literature of the time in form and content. My primary interest, by contrast, is the canonical text itself as tradition has handed it down.

I thus operate with this threefold question: What is the message of salvation—the "good news"—proclaimed by the text? How does that message draw from, and find fulfillment in, the biblical canon? And how is that message relevant to our situation? Although scholarly criticism does help to address these questions, it cannot suffice for a starting point. Scholarly criticism, in the interest of objectivity, attempts to "bracket" or "suspend" the meaning of the message as grasped *by faith*. Yet it is that very meaning of the text—the meaning intended when one *sings* the canticles or *prays* the psalms or *proclaims* the gospel—that I pursue. Instead of scholarly criticism, my primary hermeneutic is the traditional method of reading Scripture "confessionally" and "interpreting Scripture with Scripture." This traditional method is apropos of the songs and stories of Luke's gospel. These texts recollect and rearticulate—and thereby revive and reinterpret—the ancient Scriptures that not only carry the people's memory and faith in God's salvation but also project the hope of the people for freedom, justice, and peace. My style of writing also emerges from the texts themselves and is thus confessional and devotional, meditative and imaginative.

Thanks are due to four institutions that have played significant roles in the conception and execution of this book. First, to Anabaptist Mennonite Biblical Seminary in Elkhart, Indiana, where I undertook studies in Bible and theology and learned how to open both mind and heart to the Scriptures. Second, to the Benedictine community of Saint Gregory's Abbey in Three Rivers, Michigan, where over five Advent/Christmas retreats I meditated and wrote on the Lukan canticles and nativity narrative. Third, to Bridgefolk, the Mennonite-Catholic organization based at Saint John's Abbey in Collegeville, Minnesota, which promotes ecumenical exchange between Mennonite and Catholic traditions. And, fourth, to Liturgical Press, whose mission of serving the church resonates both with my own vocation and with the tenor of this book.

Finally, special thanks to four persons without whom this book might never have been written or published: Sr. Judith Anne Beatty, CSC, who directed me to the Benedictine practice of prayer; Prof. Mary Schertz, whose seminary course on Luke-Acts was both informative and formative of my reading of

Scripture; Rev. Janice Yordy Sutter, who read an early version of this book and found it helpful for Advent sermon preparation; and Prof. Michael Patella, OSB, who took interest in this project and supported its publication.

For the good of the church,
To the glory of God!

Darrin W. Snyder Belousek
Advent 2012

1

GOOD NEWS

Herald of Salvation

The good news of salvation proclaimed by and fulfilled in Jesus, whom Christians confess as Messiah and follow as Lord, was not an entirely new message with what are traditionally referred to as gospels—Matthew, Mark, Luke, and John. This gospel—literally, "good news"—had in many significant respects been preached and heard before in Israel and beyond. It can be found throughout the biblical canon, in the Torah, Prophets, and Psalms—as Jesus himself taught his disciples after the resurrection (Luke 24:27, 44-45), as Philip explained to the Ethiopian (Acts 8:35), and as the apostle Paul later testified (Acts 28:23; Rom 3:21-22). To introduce our study in the Gospel of Luke, we will take time to hear and reflect on this "gospel before the gospels." By doing so, we will not only prepare our eyes to see, our ears to hear, and our hearts to respond to the good news in Luke's narrative; we will also find that the message of salvation preached by the evangelist is one with the message proclaimed by prophet and poet. We will also discover that the good news of salvation is not static, but dynamic. Gospel is the redemptive presence and renewing power of God in history (cf. Isa 65:17-25; Rom 1:16; 2 Cor 5:17). God's good news moves in history: it is announced, received, reimaged and reworded, passed along, expanded and elaborated, proclaimed anew, handed down from messenger to hearer, who takes up the message, and so on. Indeed, in a sense, God's good news itself moves history, marking history and making history. Gospel opens history to the initiative of God and opens the human heart to respond to the divine initiative within history, so that heaven, humanity, and history—indeed, all things—might be gathered together in fullness through Christ (cf. Eph 1:8-10; Col 1:19-20).

God's Messenger of Salvation

We are introduced to God's messenger of good news, and hear the good news of salvation proclaimed, in Second Isaiah (Isa 40–66). The prophet in Isaiah announces the "consolation of Israel," the visitation of God to his people exiled in Babylon, and exhorts the people to have hope, take courage, and get ready for a reversal of their situation, because God is coming to redeem his people from exile and return them to the land of their ancestors. The following oracle calls our attention to God's messenger and message (Isa 52:7, 10):

> How beautiful upon the mountains
>   are the feet of the messenger who announces peace,
> who brings good news,
>   who announces salvation,
>   who says to Zion, "Your God reigns." . . .
> The Lord has bared his holy arm
>   before the eyes of all the nations;
> and all the ends of the earth shall see
>   the salvation of our God.

This oracle unfolds the manifold message of God. God's messenger comes with a fourfold word (v. 7):

announces	peace
brings	good news
announces	salvation
says to Zion	"Your God reigns."

The poetic structure employs a parallel of four different, yet interrelated, words to express the core meaning of God's message: peace / good news / salvation / reign of God. Each of these words implies the others. To preach any one is to proclaim the others as well: to preach good news of God's salvation is at the same time to proclaim the peace of God's reign. So, if we attend carefully to the prophetic message, we learn that the peace of God's reign is as much at the heart of the gospel as is salvation; indeed, these are interconnected as one reality. When we hear John or Jesus proclaim "the kingdom of God is near" (Matt 3:2; 4:17; Mark 1:14-15; Luke 4:43), we thus should hear echoed, "good news of salvation and peace." And when we hear the host of heaven sing, "on earth peace among those whom [God] favors" (Luke 2:14), we thus should hear an echo, "the kingdom of God is near." The heavenly host, John, and Jesus all proclaim the same message as the prophet in Isaiah.

The prophetic oracle also sounds another key theme of God's message to us: the good news of salvation and the peace of God's reign is to be revealed "before the eyes of all nations" so that "all the ends of the earth shall see the salvation of our God" (Isa 52:10). The heavenly messenger brings good news of salvation not for us only but for "all the nations" so that the peace of God's reign (= "the salvation of our God") might extend to "all the ends of the earth." The saving peace proclaimed by God's messenger is to be a universal peace, a peace in which all nations are invited to share (cf. Isa 2:2-4).

These two themes of the prophetic oracle—the unified meaning of the message of God's salvation and the universally extended scope of that message—provide crucial criteria by which we can interpret and test any message that claims to be gospel, good news from heaven. First, any message that attempts to separate or differentiate "the salvation of God" from "the peace of God's reign" is a false message, a counter-gospel: "peace," "salvation," and "the reign of God" are all *one* message, *one* proclamation, *one* gospel. To preach salvation to the exclusion of calling people into the way of peace, or to proclaim peace without calling people to repent and enter the kingdom of God, is to expose oneself as a false prophet. The way of peace *is* the way of salvation, and the reign of God *is* the foundation of all that can be truly named as "peace." Second, to proclaim God's good news for one select people to the exclusion of other peoples instead of to all peoples equally is again to proclaim a false message, a counter-gospel: the one message is for the peoples of *all* nations. The blessing of God's peace does not favor the strongest nation whose interest the weaker nations must serve; God's grace does not grant one nation the right to rule over or dominate others. Instead, God's peace is offered to all nations alike, and all nations are equally called to be subject to God's rule (cf. Isa 2:2-4). Thus, to presume that God's salvation privileges uniquely one nation to be the singularly important agent of divine purpose in history, instead of God being present to and moving through peoples of all nations, is also to expose oneself as a false prophet: there is *one* salvation, *one* peace, *one* reign of God for "anyone who fears him and does what is right" (Acts 10:35).

Given the unity and universality of God's message, we should nonetheless see from this prophetic oracle that the salvation and peace of God's reign come to us in a particular way. God's salvation is revealed in our sight through the historical redemption of Jerusalem and the deliverance of his chosen people Israel. And this salvation in history is made known to the peoples of all nations through the very voice of the particular people God has redeemed, who erupt in joyful song at the appearing of God's salvation that restores peace to the people (Isa 52:8-9):

> Listen! Your sentinels lift up their voices,
>   together they sing for joy;
> for in plain sight they see
>   the return of the LORD to Zion.

Break forth together in singing,
  you ruins of Jerusalem;
for the LORD has comforted his people,
  he has redeemed Jerusalem.

Here, again, we see parallel words of salvation in the poetic structure:

the return of the LORD to Zion
the LORD has comforted his people
the LORD has redeemed Jerusalem.

The saving act by which the people of God are delivered from exile and captivity, and by which God's peace is delivered to his people, is variously named by the prophet "visitation," "comfort," and "redemption." We will find Luke using the same words to describe aspects of God's salvation and peace in the advent of Jesus the Messiah. God's salvation is both historical and particular; God's salvation moves in history through a particular people in concrete circumstances. The particularity and historicity of the sign by which the good news is made known to us—the return of the people of Israel from exile in Babylon—tell us that God's saving peace is both spiritual and social. The "visitation" of the Lord signifies a restoration not only of the spiritual lives of individuals but also of the people as a people, so that it is the "ruins of Jerusalem"—the exiled remnant of God's people—that should "break forth *together* into singing." Thus, "visitation," "comfort," and "redemption," as words denoting God's act of salvation, have political implication that concerns the liberation of an oppressed people from captivity by a stronger nation (Isa 52:1-6). The scope of God's salvation includes the destiny of a whole people secured together in peace within their city (Isa 60–62). God's salvation, which is (to be) fulfilled *in history*, is *corporate* as well as personal, encompassing the freedom of peoples and the peace of cities as well as the spiritual security of individuals.

This oracle of good news is closely related to a complementary oracle (Isa 40:9-11):

> Get you up to a high mountain,
>   O Zion, herald of good tidings;
> lift up your voice with strength,
>   O Jerusalem, herald of good tidings,
>   lift it up, do not fear;
> say to the cities of Judah,
>   "Here is your God!"
> See, the Lord GOD comes with might,
>   and his arm rules for him;
> his reward is with him,
>   and his recompense before him.
> He will feed his flock like a shepherd;
>   he will gather the lambs in his arms,
> and carry them in his bosom,
>   and gently lead the mother sheep.

This text resonates with the themes we have seen before. First, the message of "good tidings" (= good news) is to be proclaimed from a "high mountain" so that the message may be spread far and wide rather than be kept close, so that all the peoples may hear the good news. Who is the messenger that is to proclaim good tidings from the mountaintop? The herald of good tidings is Zion/Jerusalem: it is now the *people*, the faithful remnant restored and secured within their city, who are God's messenger of salvation and peace, who lift up their voice to proclaim good tidings to the "cities of Judah." Thus, again, we see that it is the corporate salvation of God's people and the peace of their city that testify to the good news of God's salvation. And what is the word of good tidings? "Here is your God!" (v. 10)—God is with us! This word of salvation is a parallel expression to "the return of the LORD to Zion," "the LORD has comforted his people," and "the LORD has redeemed Jerusalem" that we saw in Isaiah 52:8-9. Salvation is accomplished by the redeeming presence of God to his people that restores them as God's people of peace and praise; indeed, the presence of God *is* salvation.

We see further the effects of God's salvation, referred to here as God's "reward" and "recompense" (Luke 40:10). God's salvation does not bring punishment, however much deserved, to the people; for, as the prophet has declared earlier, the time of their suffering and oppression is at an end (Isa 40:1-2). Salvation is deliverance from punishing suffering and oppression. Now is a time for restoration and renewal, a time in which the people will enjoy God's blessing. Again, just as the subject of salvation is corporate (the people of Jerusalem and the cities of Judah), so also are the benefits of salvation social. By his redemption act in history, God renews and reclaims "his flock" (Luke 40:11), which is not just a collection of individuals but a people. God saves a gathered body, a corporate entity, a "we" in which each "I" identifies with the same Shepherd; for he calls all of them by, and shepherds them under, the same name—Jacob/Israel (Isa 43:1). The corporate character of salvation carries over into the plural language used to describe the benefits of salvation. In redeeming his people, God will "feed his flock," "gather the lambs," "carry them," "lead the mother sheep" (v. 11). The protection and provision of God for his people, and their following in God's way under God's leading, are the social benefits of God's salvation.

We should notice that this salvation is by God's strength, not the people's—"the Lord God comes with might, / and his arm rules for him" (v. 10). The salvation of the people and the benefits of that salvation are worked through God's power so that this salvation is by grace, a compassionate response by God to the suffering and oppression of his people (recall the message of "comfort" and "speak tenderly" in Isa 40:1-2). The strength of the people participates in God's salvation through the proclamation of the good news in response to the peace God has delivered—"lift up your voice with strength, / O Jerusalem, herald of good tidings" (v. 9). We should notice also the interplay between the particularity of the realization of God's salvation in history and the universality of its fulfillment. The good tidings that the herald is to proclaim is addressed "to the cities of Judah" (v. 9), the cities of the people who are called by the name Jacob/

Israel. Yet this salvation, and the news of it, have a broader scope than these cities alone; the redemption of Zion/Jerusalem has universal meaning for the peoples of all nations (Isa 40:3-5). The way of salvation that God demonstrates by his power through the redemption of Israel from captivity and oppression is the way of salvation for the peoples of all nations.

Although God's salvation is to be revealed to the peoples of all nations, not everyone will enter into God's peace. A further oracle of good news to Israel in exile will illustrate the point (Isa 48:20-22):

> Go out from Babylon, flee from Chaldea,
> declare this with a shout of joy, proclaim it,
> send it forth to the end of the earth;
> say, "The LORD has redeemed his servant Jacob!"
> They did not thirst when he led them through the deserts;
> he made water flow for them from the rock;
> he split open the rock and the water gushed out.
> "There is no peace," says the LORD, "for the wicked."

The salvation message of this oracle echoes that of earlier oracles, "The LORD has redeemed his servant Jacob!" In relaying this good news of redemption, the messenger recalls God's founding act of salvation through the exodus from Egypt, in which God provided for and protected Israel in the desert as they were led forth from slavery to freedom. This messenger, however, does not carry favorable news to everyone: the messenger is sent out "with a shout of joy" to publish the news "to the end of the earth" that "[t]here is no peace . . . for the wicked." We hear a parallel message in a similar prophetic oracle (Isa 57:19-21):

> Peace, peace to the far and the near, says the LORD;
> and I will heal them.
> But the wicked are like the tossing sea
> that cannot keep still;
> its waters toss up mire and mud.
> There is no peace, says my God, for the wicked.

The prophet announces the word of God: "Peace," a word that brings healing (57:18), a word of restoration (v. 14), revival (v. 15), forgiveness (vv. 16-17), and comfort (v. 18). And this good news goes out "to the far and the near," to the people of God taken captive into exile and to the remnant of God's people left behind in Judah, both of whom await God's salvation. But this word, "Peace," is not for the wicked, who restlessly churn up muck by deeds of injustice and unrighteousness that pollute the nations. For the wicked, God has no word of peace apart from repentance.

The implication of these oracles is that the salvation of God's people from oppression and captivity comes at the expense of the imperial peace—the *Pax Babylonia*, if you will. The liberation of God's people from slavery in Egypt had come at the expense of not only the destruction of Pharaoh's army but also the devastation of rivers, crops, livestock, and even children. The "unpeace" that the imperial power had forcibly imposed upon the people of Israel was rebounded back upon the people of Egypt through the awesome display of God's command over creation. The destruction that Egypt had brought upon the people of Israel now fell as judgment upon Egypt: Pharaoh and his people now reaped the harvest of violence that they had sown through policies of injustice and practices of oppression. The liberation of God through the exodus thus overturned the domination system—the *Pax Egyptia*—by freeing the slaves upon whose backs were built Egypt's great cities and monuments and whose forced labor in the fields supported the prospering economy. Now, says the messenger in Isaiah, it will be the same for Babylon, the empire that has taken Israel captive into exile, forcing the people of God to labor for the profit of the imperial system. But instead of the powers of creation at God's command bringing "unpeace" upon Babylon, this time it will be military forces commanded by Babylon's new rival, Cyrus, king of Persia, who will overturn the *Pax Babylonia*: "he shall perform his purpose on Babylon, / and his arm shall be against the Chaldeans . . . and he will prosper in his way" (Isa 48:14-15).

God's salvation to the peoples of all nations is not "neutral" or "even-handed," but favors the oppressed, those captive to imperial powers, and overturns the systems of domination that exile, exploit, and enslave. And those who would oppose and resist God's liberation, who would oppress the poor and remain unrepentant at the Lord's coming, will find no peace though they may flee to the ends of the earth to escape God's judgment. This, then, provides another criterion, in addition to unity and universality, by which we should test the gospel we preach and hear. Good news of salvation and peace unaccompanied by warning of judgment to come is a false gospel; a message of "peace, peace" when there is no peace is not good news at all, but only serves to expose the false prophet (Jer 6:14; 8:11).

Finally, the prophet offers us a vision of the fullness of God's good news of salvation, the liberating movement of God's word in history brought full circle (Isa 55:10-12):

> For as the rain and the snow come down from heaven,
>   and do not return there until they have watered the earth,
> making it bring forth and sprout,
>   giving seed to the sower and bread to the eater,
> so shall my word be that goes out from my mouth;
>   it shall not return to me empty,
> but it shall accomplish that which I purpose,
>   and succeed in the thing for which I sent it.
> For you shall go out in joy,
>   and be led back in peace;
> the mountains and the hills before you
>   shall burst into song,
>   and all the trees of the field shall clap their hands.

The word of God, sent forth on a mission, has completed the circuit of its journey and accomplished the purpose for which it was sent. This purpose is to bring forth a new day in which the blessing of heaven falls to earth, giving new life to the earth and satisfying sustenance to the people, a day of joy and peace, song and dance. We might see in the imagery here—the people "going out in joy" and "being led back in peace," "mountains and hills bursting into song" and "trees of the field clapping their hands"—a liturgy of thanksgiving and praise to God. This imaginative language depicts the people moving outward from the sanctuary (the dwelling place of God's presence) in a procession of joy that celebrates the gift of God's word sent forth from heaven; this liturgical movement then turns back into the sanctuary in a procession announcing the peace that is accomplished by the sent word, which now returns in its fullness to God. All along the processional path the people gathered in worship ("trees of the field"), the great and the small together ("mountains and hills"), offer their song of praise to God and clap their hands in adulation of God. In this liturgy, the people return blessing to God, thanks and praise in response to the generous gift of God's word, which has descended upon and come among God's people on earth to accomplish God's purpose. The liturgical procession celebrates the fullness of God's redemption of his people; and God's word is fulfilled precisely in making his people a people of peace and praise. God's saving word is thus brought to completion in worship, the culmination of which is peace.

God's Message of Salvation

We now want to further plumb the depths of God's message of salvation. This message is rendered beautifully by the poet (Ps 85:8-13, New Jerusalem Bible):

> I am listening. What is God's message?
> Yahweh's message is peace
> for his people, for his faithful,
> if only they renounce their folly.
> His saving help is near for those who fear him,
> his glory will dwell in our land.
> Faithful Love and Loyalty join together,
> Saving Justice and Peace embrace.

> Loyalty will spring up from the earth,
> and Justice will lean down from heaven.
> Yahweh will himself give prosperity,
> and our soil will yield its harvest.
> Justice will walk before him,
> treading out a path.

God's message calls us, first, to open our ears to God's word; and to hear God's word, we must first incline our hearts in a posture of submission to God, a posture of readiness to receive and respond to God's word: "I am listening." What motivates such a posture of submission, what opens the ears and inclines the heart to God's word, is anticipation of the word that God will speak, expectation of good news: "What is God's message?" Our anticipation is then fulfilled by God's word: "Yahweh's message is peace." This message carries a twofold connotation: God speaks "Peace" to us, and God's word to us is peace. This means that God's word both signifies and constitutes peace; it both points the way to peace and is itself the way of peace. For God's word is the sacrament, the sign and reality, of peace: the word of God, which speaks peace, *is* peace. And thus those who receive God's word of peace and respond faithfully to it *already* have peace, already see over the horizon of history to the coming fulfillment of God's kingdom, already possess a measure of the fullness of God's salvation.

To receive peace, we must hear the gospel; and to hear the gospel, we must incline our hearts to God: hearing begins in the heart. We are to incline our hearts to the saving word of God because that word is a message of peace, a message that satisfies the deepest longing and highest hope of our mortal souls. To incline our hearts toward the good news of God's saving word of peace, however, we must at the same time turn away from our iniquity and sin. Where the New Revised Standard Version (NRSV) reads in verse 8, "the LORD . . . will speak peace . . . to those who turn to him in their hearts," the New Jerusalem Bible (NJB) reads, "Yahweh's message is peace . . . if only they renounce their folly." To "turn to [God] in [our] hearts" is nothing less than to "renounce [our] folly." The appropriate response to God's saving word is that we repent of our ways that war against God's reign of justice and peace.

For whom is this message? The same question could be asked, Who is prepared to receive the word of God? The poetic structure of the psalm offers us another set of parallels in answer to this question. God speaks a saving word to his people / his faithful / those who turn to him in their hearts / those who fear him (vv. 8-9). The people of God, to whom and for whom God speaks, are those who are ready and willing to hear God's word, who have turned away from sin and injustice, and have inclined their hearts to God so that they are prepared to receive the salvation and peace God will grant. And those who are prepared to receive the saving word of peace are just those who are faithful to God, who not only hear the message but also bind themselves wholly—with mind and heart, soul and might—to God's word in trust and obedience (cf. Matt 7:21-27; Luke 6:46-49). These faithful—who hear God's word, entrust their whole lives to it, and diligently follow that word—are those who "fear God." To fear God is to know before whom one stands, to revere God, and God alone, as the ultimate source of life and truth and blessing, to acknowledge God's will as the unique landmark by which to orient the life of God's people. So, we see that God's salvation and peace is offered to those who have prepared to receive it through repentance, and whose conversion is founded upon the twin pillars of trust in God alone for salvation and obedience to God's word above all else.

Now, God's salvation and peace "is near for those who fear him" (Ps 85:9). That it is "near" signifies that it may be either received or rejected by us, either taken up or left aside: though God's salvation and peace is "near," we are free to either enter into or turn away from it. God's peace is freely granted, a gift—not a reciprocal exchange or mutual contract that merely renders what is owed to us by right. And it is precisely because God's salvation and peace is by grace, that God speaks to us the saving word of peace instead of a message of wrath and condemnation despite our iniquity and sin (vv. 1-7), that "his glory will dwell in our land" (v. 9). The "peace" that is the work of our own hands—provided by our wealth and protected by our weapons at the expense of the peace of others who are deprived by our wealth or destroyed by our weapons—is nothing but "salvation by works," which produces boasting and self-glorification (cf. Eph 2:8-9). Indeed, that is the very "folly" that we are called to renounce—trying to save ourselves, to maintain our present and guarantee our future against all threats, by recourse to the false security of wealth or weapons (cf. Pss 49 and 33:10-22). That God's peace comes to "those who fear him," to those who trust in God alone for security and salvation, means that only God may be glorified thereby.

Here we understand the ultimate purpose of God's salvation—that God, and God alone, might be glorified, so that God's glory might dwell with us (Isa 60; Rev 21). Any turning of "our peace" to self-exaltation or self-congratulation, any claim that *we* are the ultimate guarantors of our own security or that the security of "our nation" is the ultimate purpose, any naming of ourselves as "peacemaker" apart from the grace of God, is pride and presumption amounting to only self-glorification. Thus, to seek "peace through strength" apart from the grace of God, through either economic prosperity or military power, is implicitly to reject God's salvation and, hence, to banish God's glory from our land.

We come now to the heart of the message. In the fullness of God's salvation, "Steadfast love and faithfulness will meet" (Ps 85:10, NRSV), "Faithful Love and Loyalty join together" (NJB). Salvation is present where God's "steadfast/faithful love" meets our "faithfulness/loyalty." God's love is steady, sturdy, and constant, ever present, always extended to us no matter how far from that love we think we have wandered or fled, offering hope to us no matter how deep our despair, inviting us home no matter how hardened our hearts may have become. We have only to turn and receive God's saving help, for God's "steadfast love" is always already there for us; it is "near." And where we turn in faithfulness, in repentance and trusting obedience to God's word of truth for us, in loyalty to God's covenant of peace with us, then there, in the meeting of our faithfulness and God's steadfast love, *is* salvation.

In the fullness of God's salvation, "Saving Justice and Peace embrace" (v. 10, NJB), "righteousness and peace will kiss each other" (NRSV). The image rendered by the poet is that God's salvation is fulfilled in the "marriage" or holy union of justice/righteousness and peace. There is to be no divorcing of justice from peace in the fulfillment of God's salvation. Ultimately, in God's salvation, justice and peace are and ever remain intimately related, united in God's steadfast love—and what God has joined together, we ought to not put asunder.

When we hear "peace" spoken by the Hebrew prophet or poet, we should hear *shalom*. *Shalom* is not merely "spiritual tranquility" or "mental repose"—an "interior peace" that all of us possess "in our hearts." For the prophets and poets of Israel, *shalom* is always outwardly visible in its manifestation and tangibly concrete in its particulars; it is always embodied in both personal and social realities, always incarnate in human lives and communities. The prophet Zechariah depicts the peace of God as a reality that binds humans to heaven, humans to one another, and humans to the earth in relationships of faithfulness and fruitfulness (Zech 8:12):

> For there shall be a sowing of peace; the vine shall yield its fruit, the ground shall give its produce, and the skies shall give their dew; and I will cause the remnant of this people to possess all these things.

The prophet Micah describes the peace of God, founded upon God's teaching and justice, as a reality that transforms economic activity, political relations, and the human psyche. God's peace is present when all peoples and nations share equally in prosperity and security (Mic 4:3-4):

> [T]hey shall beat their swords into plowshares,
> and their spears into pruning hooks;
> nation shall not lift up sword against nation,
> neither shall they learn war any more;
> but they shall all sit under their own vines and under their own fig trees,
> and no one shall make them afraid.

That God's peace is concrete in substance and social in character is why one may pronounce "*Shalom*!" upon both persons and cities (Ps 122:6-8). The Hebrew *shalom* thus signifies far more than simply the cessation of hostility or the absence of violence. It is much richer and deeper than the Latin *pax*, which signifies a "peace treaty" that, for the time being, halts a state of war between combatants.

Shalom encompasses all of lived reality—spirit and flesh, individual and community, heaven and earth, eternity and history. *Shalom* implies the comprehensive well-being or welfare of both persons and society—spiritual, psychical, physical, social, economic, political, and environmental well-being. *Shalom* signifies a fundamentally "right" or "just" situation in which everything takes its proper place and functions properly within the divinely created order. It implies right relationship—each person with him- or herself, human beings with one another, humans with the earth, and humanity with God. *Shalom* is thus a situation of harmony and wholeness in which God's original creative intention is fulfilled or realized in concrete terms. *Shalom* is tangibly present when everyone from the least to the greatest enjoys sufficiency of basic goods, when everyone from the weakest to the strongest is sustained in life-giving relationships of mutuality and equality, where fundamental rights and responsibilities are respected and fulfilled.

Thus, in the vision of the Hebrew prophets and poets, all that can be truly named as peace necessarily includes justice. And justice requires not only equality and fairness for all persons; it also requires preferential provision and protection for the poor, weak, and vulnerable—"the alien, widow, and orphan" and the "blind, oppressed, and imprisoned" that are so often mentioned by the prophets and poets because they are of special concern to God (cf. Ps 146; Isa 61). Justice, therefore, always has as its proper aim restoring or creating *shalom*: restoring a situation that is "right" in its basic elements according to what God has ordained; righting wrong by redeeming what human beings have broken, denied, or stolen. Justice seeks to honor God by respecting God's image. Hence, where human dignity is violated, justice is trampled; and where justice is trampled, peace is exiled. Where the rights of some are denied due to the pride or prejudice or ambition or avarice of others, there is no peace; where the basic needs of some go unmet due to the greed or gluttony or blindness or indifference of others, there is no peace. "Peace" without justice for the poor, weak, and vulnerable is merely the comfortableness of the status quo, the tranquility of the existing order, a "peace" that rings hollow. Such a "peace" that ignores the needs of the hungry, homeless, and naked, or abrogates the rights of the foreigner and the prisoner, whether in the name of "freedom" or "security," is ultimately a rejection of the reign of God (Matt 25:31-46).

Likewise, justice without peace is ultimately empty; for, indeed, peace is the fulfillment, the goal of all that can be truly named as justice. We ought to pursue justice, but we cannot, in fidelity to God's salvation, pursue justice by any means destructive of peace; for by doing so we destroy the very end that gives meaning and motivation to our pursuit. In God's salvation there must be a marriage of means and ends, of justice and peace; for the end is contained within the means, and vice versa. This is the wisdom of gospel: "all who take the sword will perish by the sword" (Matt 26:52), but "a harvest of justice is sown in peace for those who make peace" (Jas 3:18). To pursue justice by violent or alienating means is to pursue a false justice, and to pursue peace by means that violate human rights is to pursue a false peace. True peace, the peace of God, cannot be secured or saved by war; and true justice, justice that restores or creates peace, cannot be served by retributive violence that imitates the peace-destroying injustice that begs to be righted.

This marriage of means and ends, justice and peace, articulated within the poet's image of God's salvation, is also revealed by the prophet. In Isaiah 59, the prophet depicts a society that is corrupt to the core, a city that is ruled by lies and violence, where deception and bloodshed are rampant, where the innocent and weak are crushed. The people of the city "wait for justice, but there is none; / for salvation, but it is far from us" (Isa 59:11). Due to the iniquity of the people, truth is raped by the elected officials while the news reporters look on nodding their approval; justice is served an injunction by the courts and then deported from the city by the immigration officials (v. 14):

> Justice is turned back,
>   and righteousness stands at a distance;
> for truth stumbles in the public square,
>   and uprightness cannot enter.

The prophet diagnosed why there is an absence of justice and peace (vv. 8-9):

> The way of peace they do not know,
>   and there is no justice in their paths.
> Their roads they have made crooked;
>   no one who walks in them knows peace.
> Therefore justice is far from us,
>   and righteousness does not reach us.

The reason "justice is far from" the people is because "[t]he way of peace they do not know." The ways of the people lack justice because the people do not know the way of peace; and, conversely, the people do not know peace because they follow the path of injustice ("crooked roads"). There is an oft-quoted exhortation from Pope Paul VI: "If you want peace, work for justice" (cf. Isa 32:17). The poet and prophet also proclaim the transposed exhortation: If you want justice, seek peace and pursue it (cf. Ps 34:11-14).

Let us return to Psalm 85. What is the full effect of God's salvation, in which faithfulness meets steadfast love and saving justice embraces peace? When we are secured together in peace by relationships of faithfulness and justice, then our relationship with heaven is itself righted and we are at peace with God: "Faithfulness will spring up from the ground, / and righteousness will look down from the sky" (v. 11, NRSV). Thus, the salvation and peace of God encompasses both our "horizontal" relationships with one another and our "vertical" relationship with God. We cannot stand in right relationship with God apart from seeking to be faithful to one another in loving relationships of peace and justice that are founded upon trusting obedience to God's word. God's salvation is fulfilled, fully present among us, only when relationships are righted—there is "justification" and "reconciliation"—along both horizontal and vertical dimensions. To repair peace with God, therefore, we must repair peace with one other (cf. Matt 5:23-24).

This fullness of God's salvation imparts not only the peace of reconciliation but also the blessing of abundance: "The LORD will give what is good, / and our land will yield its increase" (Ps 85:12, NRSV). In the fullness of God's peace, there is enough for everyone; and because God has ordained our abundance, everyone can afford to be generous so that it is unnecessary for anyone to be deprived of what they need. God's salvation thus engenders an economy of abundance rather than scarcity, an economy of mutual interdependence rather than individualistic competition, an economy of openhanded sharing with others rather than tightfisted keeping for oneself (cf. Luke 6:30-31; 12:16-34; Acts 2:44-45; 4:32-37). Just as we enjoy right relationship with God when we pursue right relationship with others, so, too, do we enjoy God's blessing when we seek to practice the economy of abundance and generosity toward others. In all this, both when we practice right relationships of peace and justice and when we practice the economy of abundance and generosity, we follow in the path of salvation that God prepares before us (Ps 85:13).

From the Good News of Isaiah to the Gospel of Luke

Before turning to reflect on the Gospel of Luke, it will be instructive to make explicit the bridge between the prophetic word of good news and the Messiah whose advent proclaimed in the gospels brings that word to fulfillment. Luke's narrative of the good news of salvation revealed in Jesus draws explicitly in significant ways upon the prophet Isaiah. In particular, Luke 1–4 (and, to a significant extent, Luke's entire narrative of Jesus) is patterned after the prophetic oracle with which we began, Isaiah 52:7—

> How beautiful upon the mountains
> are the feet of the messenger who announces peace,
> who brings good news,
>   who announces salvation,
>   who says to Zion, "Your God reigns."

As we developed in detail above, this prophetic oracle unfolds the fourfold word of God's message to the people: peace, good news, salvation, and reign of God. These four words are sounded with vigor and joy in Luke's nativity narrative, and resound throughout Luke's gospel, so that it is evident that Luke understands Jesus to be the ultimate fulfillment of the prophetic message. We will unfold the links between the prophetic message of Isaiah 52:7 and the thematic threads of Luke 1–4.

Good News

1:17-19—Zechariah receives "*good news*" from God via the messenger Gabriel, who announces the birth of a forerunner of the Messiah (cf. 1:76; 3:4).

2:10-11—The Lord's messenger announces to the shepherds "*good news* of great joy for all the people" concerning the birth of "a Savior, who is the Messiah, the Lord."

3:18—Prior to Jesus' baptism and inaugural sermon, John "proclaimed *good news* to the people," a description that parallels the earlier statement that John was "proclaiming a baptism of repentance for the forgiveness of sins" (3:3; cf. 1:77).

4:18-19—In his inaugural sermon at the synagogue in Nazareth, Jesus begins his mission by announcing that he is anointed by the Spirit of the Lord "to bring *good news* to the poor." Later, when John sends his disciples to ask Jesus whether he might be "the one" (i.e., the Messiah), Jesus sends back the confirming word that "the poor have *good news* brought to them" (7:22).

4:43—After a period of ministry in Capernaum, Jesus resolves to carry his mission to the rest of Galilee, saying, "I must proclaim the *good news* of the kingdom of God to the other cities also; for I was sent for this purpose."

Salvation

1:47—Mary, after the annunciation by the angel that she would bear a holy child, the Son of God, goes to visit her cousin Elizabeth; after greeting Elizabeth and receiving a blessing in return, Mary sings of "God my *Savior*."

1:68, 71—At the circumcision and naming of John, Zechariah sings that God has "raised up a mighty *savior* for us" in order to fulfill the promise "that we would be *saved* from our enemies and from the hand of all who hate us." He then blesses John as the one who "will go before the Lord . . . to give knowledge of *salvation* to his people / by the forgiveness of their sins" (1:76-77).

2:11—The angel announces to the shepherds the birth of "a *Savior*, who is the Messiah, the Lord."

2:30-31—Simeon, upon seeing the child-Messiah, sings that "my eyes have seen your *salvation*, / which you have prepared in the presence of all peoples."

3:4-6—John, quoting Isaiah, announces that "all flesh shall see the *salvation* of God" once "the way of the Lord" has been prepared (cf. 1:77). Later, when Zacchaeus repents of his injustice, makes restitution, and distributes his wealth to the poor, Jesus announces, "Today *salvation* has come to this house" (19:9).

Peace

1:79—Zechariah sings that the advent of the Messiah is a dawn breaking from above that is "to guide our feet into the way of *peace*."

2:14—After the messenger announces to the shepherds the "good news" that the Savior, Messiah and Lord, has been born, the heavenly host praises God, saying "Glory to God in the highest heaven, / and on earth *peace* among those whom he favors!" This heavenly hymn of peace is answered by the disciples' earthly hymn of peace as Jesus enters Jerusalem (19:38). Thus, the advent of the Messiah to Israel, culminating in the visitation of the Messiah to Jerusalem, is framed by hymns of peace: "the way of the Lord" (3:4) is none other than "the way of *peace*" (1:79). This is why Jesus laments over Jerusalem, because the city has failed to recognize "the way to *peace*" (19:42, NJB).

2:29—Upon seeing the Messiah as promised, Simeon sings, "Master, now you are dismissing your servant in *peace*, / according to your word." Later, Jesus sends forth two women, one forgiven of her sin and the other healed of her bleeding, with the word, "go in *peace*" (7:50; 8:48).

Reign/Kingdom of God

1:32-33—Gabriel tells Mary that God will give her promised child, the "Son of God," "the throne of his ancestor David" and that "[h]e will *reign* over the house of Jacob forever, and of his *kingdom* there will be no end."

2:11—The angel's announcement of Jesus' birth proclaims that this Savior is Messiah (*Christos*, the one anointed or chosen by God to rule) and Lord (*kyrios*, sovereign over his kingdom).

4:43—Jesus says to the crowd that the very purpose for which he has been sent is to "proclaim the good news of the *kingdom of God*." This theme—proclaiming the good news of the kingdom of God—resounds throughout Luke's narrative of Jesus; it characterizes both the mission of Jesus and the mission on which he sends his disciples (cf. 8:1; 9:2, 11; 9:60; 11:2; 11:20; 12:32; 13:29; 14:15; 16:16; 17:21; 18:17, 24, 29; 19:38; 22:29-30; 23:51). When Jesus sends the seventy into the towns and villages on the way to Jerusalem, they are instructed to greet each house they enter with "Peace" and, after sharing bread and healing the sick, to announce that "[t]he *kingdom of God* has come near" (10:5, 9). This mission to proclaim the good news of God's kingdom does not end with the resurrection and ascension of Jesus, but continues through the missionary life of the early church (Acts 8:4-5, 12, 25, 35, 40).

2

FEAR NOT

Salvation and Deliverance

The Coming of the Lord

Zechariah is a priest of the Lord; indeed, he belongs to a priestly order and is married to a descendant of Aaron, the first priest of Israel (Luke 1:5). Consecrated to serve in the presence of God, he has been trained to perform the ritual duties within the temple (v. 8). He, along with his wife Elizabeth, is "righteous before God, living blamelessly according to all the commandments and regulations of the Lord" (v. 6). One day, while performing his assigned duties, he enters "the sanctuary of the Lord" (the holy place within the temple) to offer incense while the assembly of the people prayed outside in the court (vv. 9-10). If anyone is prepared to meet God's messenger, anyone who has no cause to be terrified at God's word, it would seem to be the righteous priest Zechariah in the faithful performance of his sacred duties. "Then there appeared to him an angel of the Lord, standing at the right side of the altar of incense. When Zechariah saw him, he was terrified; and fear overwhelmed him" (vv. 11-12).

Mary is a peasant girl, a "virgin" engaged to be married; indeed, she is betrothed to no less than a descendant of David (vv. 26-27). She is apparently a virtuous young woman who has lived rightly before God, someone who knows what it means to "fear the Lord and do right." She is thus favored by God, as the angel declares (v. 28): "Greetings, favored one! The Lord is with you." If anyone is prepared to receive good news from heaven, it would seem to be the virgin Mary. "But she was much perplexed by his words" (v. 29). Here we have a classic example of understatement—"much perplexed." The NRSV translation leaves us with the impression that the angel's greeting merely presented Mary with an intellectual riddle, or simply put her in an uncustomary situation, such that she "pondered what sort of greeting this might be." The NJB translation takes us closer to the inner effect of the angel's greeting upon Mary: "She was deeply disturbed by these words." The angel's greeting was addressed not only to Mary's mind, but to her spirit, which was "deeply disturbed" by the message. The word of the messenger is not simply a strange salutation, but implicitly a disturbing existential probe into the very heart of Mary's being, a probe that prompts terrifying inner questions: Why is God coming to me? Am I adequate to God's will?

The shepherds are among the poorest of the poor, despised and outcast, existing on the margins of society. They live in the fields with the flocks they tend (2:8), flocks that likely belong to a wealthy landowner who pays them a subsistence wage. They may well have lost their own fields due to heavy indebtedness to fellow Israelites, and might even have had their own flocks once but had to sell at unfair prices in order to pay burdensome taxes to Rome. Perhaps, though, they know the law of Moses, which grants forgiveness of debts every Sabbath year (Deut 15) and return of each to his own land every Jubilee year (Lev 25); perhaps, too, they have heard of the prophet's oracle of "the year of the Lord's favor," which promises "good news to the oppressed" (Isa 61:1-2). Perhaps, then, they are hoping for the day of their vindication, when God's restoring justice appears. If anyone is prepared to see the day of God's coming, it might seem to be our humble shepherds. "Then an angel of the Lord stood before them, and the glory of the Lord shone around them, and they were terrified" (Luke 2:9).

God's messenger brings good news of salvation, but the appearance of the messenger is terrifying. The announcing of good news in our midst means that heaven is coming down to earth, God is coming near to us, the gulf between divine and mortal is closing—and that *is* terrifying. When God approaches us through his messenger, when we are drawn into an encounter with the Holy One, reverent "fear of the Lord" appropriately becomes terror as our unrighteousness is highlighted by the refining fire of God's holiness (Mal 3:1-2):

> See, I am sending my messenger to prepare the way before me, and the Lord whom you seek will suddenly come to his temple. The messenger of the covenant in whom you delight—indeed, he is coming, says the LORD of hosts. But who can endure the day of his coming, and who can stand when he appears?

In a world where the rights of the weak and vulnerable—the poor, homeless, and immigrants—are trampled by increasing tax privileges for the wealthiest, by laws banishing the destitute from public space and denying the indigent access to basic needs, and by "justice" that secretly selects and detains "suspects" without evidence because of their religion, ethnicity, and foreign origin; in a world where "the rich get richer while the poor get prison" and "those without the capital get the punishment" all the while the warehousing and exploited labor of the imprisoned poor garner ever-increasing profits for private industry; in a world in which wars of "freedom" waged by the mighty armies of the richest nations leave strewn in their wake the dead and maimed bodies of thousands upon thousands of innocent women and children among the defenseless poor of the weakest nations; in a world in which "liberty" and "privacy" are used and abused to shield from the reach of law and morality the deliberate killing of millions upon millions of the weakest and most vulnerable members of human society, the unborn—in such a world as this the coming of God *should* strike terror in our hearts, if we yet have hearts of flesh, if our hearts have not turned to stone.

The poet captures our anxious anticipation of God's coming in vivid terms (Ps 76:7-9, NJB):

> You, you alone, strike terror! Who can hold his ground
> in your presence when your anger strikes?
> From heaven your verdicts thunder,
> the earth is silent with dread
> when God takes his stand to give judgment,
> to save all the humble of the earth.

God comes with judgment "to save all the humble of the earth." Are we to be saved or judged, acquitted or sentenced? Is it really *good* news when God speaks to mortals? *For whom* is this message "good news"? The sober human response would be to flee with terror before the coming of the Lord.

But the angel said to Zechariah, "Do not be afraid . . . " (Luke 1:13).

And the angel said to Mary, "Do not be afraid . . . " (1:30).

And the angel said to the shepherds, "Do not be afraid . . . " (2:10).

The first word of God's good news, the fore-word of the gospel, is, "Fear not." Why need we not fear the message of the angel?

"But the angel said to him, 'Do not be afraid, Zechariah, for your prayer has been heard' " (1:13). God comes near to us in response to our petition of mercy—God has heard and God has responded. God is not infinitely removed and eternally immovable; God is not dispassionate and unconcerned, disinterested and unreachable. God has not forgotten our situation and we are not abandoned; God can be reached and moved to act in our world, in our time, by our intercessions. This indeed is "good news" (v. 19), and is cause not for fearfulness, but joy and praise: "Now the time came for Elizabeth to give birth, and she bore a son. Her neighbors and relatives heard that the Lord had shown his great mercy to her, and they rejoiced with her" (vv. 57-58). "Immediately [Zechariah's] mouth was opened and his tongue freed, and he began to speak, praising God" (v. 64).

"The angel said to her, 'Do not be afraid, Mary, for you have found favor with God'" (1:30). God comes near to us when we walk humbly before God, when we "fear God and do right." It is not the proud—the wise, mighty, and wealthy who boast in themselves (Jer 9:23)—to whom God comes with saving help. God looks favorably upon the humility of those who are God's servants (Luke 1:48)—those who know that God delights in "steadfast love, justice, and righteousness" (Jer 9:24). And God's "mercy is for those who fear him / from generation to generation" (Luke 1:50). This indeed is good news, and is cause not for existential crisis, but wholehearted submission to God's word and whole-lived commitment to God's service: "Here am I, the servant of the Lord; let it be with me according to your word" (v. 38).

"But the angel said to them, 'Do not be afraid; for see—I am bringing you good news of great joy for all the people'" (2:10). What about the poor and oppressed, whose only hope for vindication and justice is in the Lord? Is there "good news" for them? Or is this message only for the pious, the righteous priests and humble virgins? God responds to the petitions of, and comes near with saving help for, all those who are vulnerable and needy—the oppressed and hungry, the blind and bowed down, the stranger, orphan, and widow (Ps 146:7-9). Though many are excluded from divine grace by the self-righteous and made outcasts from social welfare by the powerful and privileged, the messenger from heaven announces "good news . . . *for all the people*." This indeed is good news, and is not cause to flee before the coming of the Lord, but to act immediately and decisively upon the message one has heard: "When the angels had left them and gone into heaven, the shepherds said to one another, 'Let us go now to Bethlehem and see this thing that has taken place, which the Lord has made known to us.' So they went with haste" (Luke 2:15-16).

Fore-Word of Good News

This fore-word of good news—"Fear not"—spoken by the angel to our main characters in Luke's story of Jesus' birth echoes the thematic pattern found in the good news announced to Israel by the prophet Isaiah. There, the good news concerns Israel's "consolation," redemption from captivity in Babylon and return from exile to the land of the ancestors (Isa 35:4; 41:14; 44:1-2, 8; 51:7, 12-13; 54:4, 14). The prophet's annunciation of "comfort" to Jerusalem (40:1-2) is followed by the prophet's call to Zion/Jerusalem to go "up to a high mountain" and be the "herald of good tidings," to "lift up your voice with strength" with the message, "Here is your God" (40:9). In the midst of this call to God's people to be the herald of good news, even before the message that God is near is revealed to the messenger, the prophet says, "lift it up, do not fear." To lift up our voice to proclaim the gospel is to be released from fearfulness.

The coming of God inspires "holy terror" among those who "fear the Lord," but at the same time God's saving presence delivers God's faithful from fearfulness. From what fear do we need deliverance? We, the prophet's audience, find ourselves in exile, removed from our homeland, without access to God through our temple (now a burned-out heap of rubble), aliens in a foreign land with neighbors that worship false gods. We are captive to an empire, powerless before a power that enslaves God's people and wars against God's peace. The situation of God's people in the story of Jesus' birth is not unlike that of Israel in exile—occupied by Roman military forces, oppressed by exploitative imperial taxation, repressed by domestic collaborating parties, barraged by pagan culture, and disheartened by temple-council corruption. There is, it would seem, much cause for God's faithful to be fearful—indeed, fear is the chief force by which the imperial power and its collaborating authorities keep the people in thralldom, submissive and reluctant to resist. The contemporary church in North America also lives in a climate of escalating fearfulness—fear of terrorism, fear of crime, fear of recession—that "justifies" increasingly repressive "security" measures and "preemptive" war. (Bear in mind that there is a significant difference between being afraid in the sense of "scared" and being afraid in the sense of "fearful." I think of that lone Chinese citizen confronting the army tank in Beijing's Tiananmen Square in 1989: he was likely scared in that situation—who wouldn't be!—but had evidently overcome fear of what the government forces might do to him.)

To those who are fearful comes this message from the prophet (Isa 41:8, 10-13):

> But you, Israel, my servant,
> Jacob, whom I have chosen . . .
> do not fear, for I am with you,
> do not be afraid, for I am your God;
> I will strengthen you, I will help you,
> I will uphold you with my victorious right hand. . . .
> You shall seek those who contend with you,
> but you shall not find them;
> those who war against you
> shall be as nothing at all.
> For I, the LORD your God,
> hold your right hand;
> it is I who say to you, "Do not fear,
> I will help you."

We need not be fearful of our enemies, those who hate us and make war against us. Nor need we be fearful of God's coming near to us, precisely because the Lord is our God, and our God is with us, and God's presence *is* our help and defense, our strength and victory. While release from fear is preparation for proclaiming good news, the good news that "I, the LORD your God, / hold your right hand" itself delivers us from fear; for the word of God proclaimed and fulfilled in our midst *is* salvation.

Although it is the advent of the protective presence of God that delivers God's faithful from fear, that God's coming delivers from fear is premised upon the covenant relationship between

God and God's people. For the coming near of God, and the proclamation of the good news of God's coming, is not only occasioned by the people's circumstance of oppression and God's zeal for justice, but is anchored deeply within both Israel's history and God's character—the calling or election of God's people, and God's faithfulness and steadfast love toward the people he has graciously called his own. God will carry us safely through the waters and the flames and will gather us in peace from the ends of the earth—hence, we need not be fearful!—because God, who has redeemed and named us as his people, is with us (Isa 43:1-5). The coming of God frees us *from* fear, and frees us *to* be the people of God, to remember God's covenant, to remember that we were created and called to be more than servants of imperial ambition, that we are pledged to the service of the Lord our God. This fore-word of good news, "Fear not," is thus a call to remembrance and reclamation, to remember and reclaim who and whose we are. And by the remembrance of our heritage and the renewal of our identity, we, the people of God, are to bear witness to the peoples and rulers of the nations that there is only one Lord and God, one Sovereign over all the earth and author of salvation (Isa 43:10-11). Having been recalled to ourselves and to our God by the word of God's messenger, we are now freed from fear to be God's witnesses, to follow with our poor shepherds and "go tell it on the mountain" that God's saving peace has come.

The birth of Jesus fulfills the prophetic oracles calling exiled Israel to "Fear not" and prepare in hope for the Lord's visitation, the advent of God's salvation: Jesus *is* the saving presence of God, sent to deliver God's people from fear to trust, from bondage to freedom, from oppression to justice. As Jesus enters Jerusalem, however, God's mission encounters resistance from a city that fails to "recognize . . . the things that make for peace . . . the time of visitation from God" and thus rejects God's peace by rejecting the Prince of Peace. This fearful, violent rejection of God's peaceful coming will one day tragically precipitate Rome's violent siege of Jerusalem (Luke 19:41-44). Yet God's mission of salvation ultimately succeeds through fear-overcoming and violence-inverting resurrection, by which God once more visits his people with salvation and peace through the risen Jesus. Jesus' resurrection appearance to the gathered disciples evokes fear: "They were startled and terrified" (24:37). Perhaps the disciples wondered as the risen Jesus stood before them: Has Jesus returned to visit God's vengeance upon us for having betrayed, denied, and deserted him? Despite their (rightful) terror, Jesus has returned to proclaim again God's good news of salvation; and the first word of good news is a fear-dispelling word, "Peace be with you" (24:36).

Fear Not, Follow Me

If we review Luke's story of Jesus' ministry, we find also that this first word of good news, "Fear not," figures crucially in Jesus' call and teaching of his disciples. The scene in which Jesus calls Peter, James, and John is set along the shore of the Sea of Galilee (5:1-11). With a crowd of folks pressing in eager "to hear the word of God" (v. 1), Jesus, seeing fishermen washing their nets beside their boats on the shore, takes the initiative by getting into the boat belonging to Simon Peter and directing him to put the boat out from shore. Assuming the traditional rabbinical teaching posture, Jesus "sat down and taught the crowds from the boat" (vv. 2-3). After ending the Torah lesson, Jesus again takes the initiative, directing Simon, "Put out into the deep water and let down your nets for a catch" (v. 4). Simon protests that they had just labored through a long night without profit, but then submits to Jesus' command: "Yet if you say so, I will let down the nets" (v. 5). The result, of course, is a net-breaking, hold-overflowing, boat-sinking catch of fish (vv. 7-8). Simon does not respond with rejoicing, however; instead he responds penitently and reverently: "he fell down at Jesus' knees, saying, 'Go away from me, Lord, for I am a sinful man!' " (v. 8).

We should see a familiar pattern here. The word of God has come near to the gathered people through the presence and teaching of Jesus. Although Simon fails at first to recognize that he is being drawn into an encounter with God's salvation through Jesus' initiative, the wonder of the great catch breaks upon his heart even as the weight of the fish breaks the nets. Just as "the glory of the Lord" told the shepherds before the angel began to speak that heaven was descending to earth, this wondrous sign reveals to Simon that he has been favored with God's visitation. Simon is duly afraid, for God's coming near exposes and judges his sin; and he instinctively seeks to remove himself from the illuminating light and refining fire of God's presence.

In the face of Simon's reverent penitence, Jesus persists in extending God's initiative: "Then Jesus said to Simon, 'Do not be afraid'" (v. 10). The first word of good news to Simon, the fore-word of salvation, is once again, "Fear not." Before Jesus can call Simon to follow him, before Simon can respond wholeheartedly to Jesus' call, Simon needs to be delivered from fear by God's word. Delivered from fear to what? "Do not be afraid; from now on you will be catching people" (v. 10). Simon is saved by God's word in Jesus, delivered from fear to serve God by extending to others the gracious invitation that he has received from God. As God's word in Jesus has brought in a great catch of fish from the depths of the sea, so, too, will God's word through Simon draw a great "catch" of people, an ingathering of folks from every nation into peace with God and one another (Acts 2 and 10). Simon, along with business partners James and John, like the shepherds before them, act immediately and decisively upon the good news they have heard in order to become partners in God's venture: "When they had brought their boats to shore, they left everything and followed him" (v. 11).

Later on, surrounded by a "crowd gathered by the thousands," Jesus "began to speak first to his disciples" (12:1). After warning them to beware the hypocrisy of the Pharisees, he says, "I tell you, my friends, do not fear those who kill the body, and after that can do nothing more. But I will warn you whom to fear: fear him who, after he has killed, has authority to cast into hell. Yes, I tell you, fear him!" (vv. 4-5). Jesus had just encountered resistance from the Pharisees and scribes, and had explicitly charged them with inheriting the blood guilt of their ancestors who had killed the prophets sent by God (11:47-50). Not surprisingly, this charge evokes hostility from the scribes and Pharisees, who now begin "lying in wait for him" (11:53). In this context, the intent of Jesus' instruction to his disciples is clear (my paraphrase): "Those who devise evil against the prophets and apostles of God are but mere mortals—the most they can do is kill the body. Do not be afraid of them. Rather, revere the One who has power and authority over both body and soul—fear God!"

Jesus continues: "Are not five sparrows sold for two pennies? Yet not one of them is forgotten in God's sight. But even the hairs of your head are all counted. Do not be afraid; you are of more value than many sparrows" (12:6-7). Those who revere God, who entrust the entirety of life, body and soul, into God's hand and for God's service, have no need to be afraid of any earthly power or human authority. For if God protects and provides for even the littlest of his creatures, then surely God will protect and provide for those who revere him and serve him faithfully, who are much more precious in his sight. This is good news!

Jesus immediately follows this fore-word of good news, "Fear not," with the word, "Do not worry." Against the same background of hostile resistance from those who are looking "to catch [Jesus] in something he might say" so that they can put him on trial for blasphemy (11:54), Jesus encourages his disciples to remain loyal to him in the event of their own arrest and trial. After pledging to acknowledge in heaven all who acknowledge him on earth, and to deny in heaven those who deny him on earth (12:8-9), Jesus promises his disciples the wisdom of the Holy Spirit during the time of trial: "When they bring you before the synagogues, the rulers, and the authorities, do not worry about how you are to defend yourselves or what you are to say; for the Holy Spirit will teach you at that very hour what you ought to say" (vv. 11-12). The "rulers and authorities" may threaten Jesus' followers with death if they do not deny Jesus, but those who revere God need not worry in facing trial on account of loyalty to Jesus, for the Holy Spirit will be their advocate and intercessor. That, too, is good news!

Strive for the Kingdom

Jesus brings together these two key words—"Fear not" and "Do not worry"—in his instruction about material needs. Having assured his disciples that God has already pledged to protect their lives, even their souls in death, Jesus tells them that they need not worry about provision for their bodies: "Therefore I tell you, do not worry about your life, what you will eat, or about your body, what you will wear. For life is more than food, and the body more than clothing" (12:22-23). The "therefore" refers us back in the text to the parable of the rich fool and the question from the crowd that prompted it. A man in the crowd demands that Jesus arbitrate a dispute between he and his brother over the family inheritance (v. 13). Jesus refuses to play the role of judge (v. 14), instead warning the crowd, "Take care! Be on your guard against all kinds of greed" (v. 15). After this he tells a parable of a rich man whose land had produced so abundantly that his barns were insufficient to hold all the harvested grain (vv. 16-20). Instead of thanking God for his abundance and sharing his grain with others in need, the rich man congratulated himself for his success and kept it all for himself. God in return demanded of the man an accounting of his life and found it wanting. Jesus concludes, "So it is with those who store up treasures for themselves but are not rich toward God" (v. 21).

What does being "rich toward God" entail? The prophet tells us that we give to God only insofar as we share our abundance with others in need (Isa 58:5-7). The moral of the parable is thus that "one's life does not consist in the abundance of one's possessions" (Luke 12:15), but rather in being generous toward others with the abundance of possessions one has. It is the depth and breadth of one's generosity, not the height and girth of one's grain or gold pile, that is the measure of one's life before God. To fail to share generously with those in need out of one's abundance is to be weightless in God's scales, to be bankrupt by God's accounting standards. The implication of this parable is that those who possess an abundance of goods—more than they *need* in basics such as shelter, food, clothing, and money—but do not share of their abundance with those lacking such necessities fail not simply to be "charitable," but fail to do *what is right*. The justice and mercy of God's kingdom (Mic 6:8; cf. Luke 6:30-36; 11:42) call for generosity in circumstances of abundance: sharing with the poor is *not optional*, but an essential response to God's salvation.

We can thus understand the "therefore" that Jesus then addresses to his disciples: "Therefore . . . do not worry about your life." If God provides for the birds of the air and the lilies of the field, which neither sow nor reap nor toil nor spin, then all the more will he provide for us, who are so much more valuable to God (12:24-28). And besides, the weight of one's life in God's scales is not counted in food or clothing, what one takes into or puts on the body, but rather by deeds of justice and mercy, what one does *with* the body for the sake of others. Because God provides generously for his own, one *need* not live in the pursuit of possessions; and because one's life in God's eyes is not measured in possessions, but rather in deeds of justice and mercy, one *ought* to not spend one's life in the pursuit of possessions. *Therefore*, "do not keep striving for what you are to eat and what you are to drink, and do not keep worrying" (v. 29). Indeed, go further than relinquishing the pursuit of possessions; because God knows what you need (v. 30), you can trust God completely for your life: "Sell your possessions, and give alms" (v. 33). The word "Do not worry" frees one from striving after possessions at the expense of the welfare of both one's soul and one's neighbor. Again, good news!

We are now ready to see the intimate connection between these two words of good news—"Fear not . . . Do not worry"—and the peace of God's kingdom, why deliverance from fearfulness and worry is crucial to receiving God's peace: "For it is the nations of the world that strive after these things" (v. 30). In speaking of "the nations" whose "striving" is opposed to the way of God's kingdom, Jesus is at this point referring implicitly to the Romans. The way of "striving" for and stockpiling the goods of the earth so that we may "relax, eat, drink, be merry" (v. 19) is precisely the way of empire. And the measure of empire is the extent of the emperor's terrestrial domain and the amount of tribute and taxes he can exact from conquered kings and subject peoples—empire is measured by the height and girth of the emperor's grain and gold piles. This way of empire, based in the economics of acquisition and accumulation (and, of course, the politics of conquest and domination), is in diametrical opposition to the way of God's kingdom, which is premised upon the economics of trust and generosity. The parable of the rich fool is effectively a judgment on empire: the emperor has reaped a great "harvest" by conquering the lands and confiscating the goods of the nations, but God has audited the emperor's books and found the imperial way to be bankrupt by the accounting standards of God's kingdom.

The imperialist economics of acquisition and accumulation wars against the peace of God's kingdom. Continual striving after land and resources, the power and treasure of earth, leads nations into incessant conflict, not because the earth's goods are scarce, but because our desires are never satisfied. Both Hebrew and Greek wisdom traditions draw the connection between insatiable "striving" and war. Recall that the parable of the rich fool followed upon Jesus' warning to the people against "greed" (v. 15). The Greek word translated "greed" is *pleonexia,* which names the vice of wanting to outdo others by gaining and having more and more without limit beyond the bounds of necessity, striving that leads inevitably to taking from others what is not one's own. In the classic tradition of Greek wisdom, this vice is opposed to the virtue of justice, which renders "to each one his own" or "to each one his due." According to both Hebrew and Greek sages, *pleonexia* leads to injustice, and greed-driven injustice is the root cause of war. In the Epistle of James, a pastoral exposition of the Hebrew wisdom and ethics reflected in the Sermon on the Mount, we read how personal *pleonexia* leads to conflict and murder (4:1-2):

> Those conflicts and disputes among you, where do they come from? Do they not come from your cravings that are at war within you? You want something and do not have it; so you commit murder. And you covet something and cannot obtain it; so you engage in disputes and conflicts.

In *The Republic* by Plato, a Greek philosophical treatise on political justice, we read how social *pleonexia* leads to one city robbing its neighbor, which provokes retaliation and results in war (372e–373e):

> We are considering not only how a city comes to be, it seems, but also a luxurious city . . . Then we must again make the city larger? For this healthy city is no longer sufficient, but must at this point be swollen in bulk and multitude with things which do not exist in cities for the sake of what is necessary . . . And the territory sufficient to sustain them then will now be insufficient and too small . . . So we must slice off some of our neighbor's land, if we are going to have enough for plow and pasture—and they in turn must take ours, if they also give themselves over to unlimited acquisition of wealth, overstepping the bounds of the necessary . . . The next thing is . . . we will be at war.[1]

Imperialist expansion is driven by the same *pleonexia*. No sooner have stronger nations conquered and occupied weaker nations than they want more, or worry that they will lose to hostile forces what they have gained at expense of blood and treasure. And thus further fear-driven wars (in which aggression is renamed "defense" or "preemption") are sure to follow, as past bloodshed justifies future bloodshed in a vicious cycle. Indeed, that is why Rome had conquered and occupied Galilee and Judea—to gain a "buffer zone" against potential threats from empires to the east and to extract wealth from the land and the people's labor through taxation. And that is why Rome spent blood and treasure to put down with ferocity and brutality every rebellion by the Jewish people (eventually razing Jerusalem and scattering the population) in order to maintain iron-fisted rule over the territory. So it was that the so-called *Pax Romana* was in fact a perpetual war.

In the twentieth century, economically structured *pleonexia* was the driving force behind no less than three covert "wars of consumption" waged by the Central Intelligence Agency of the United States to protect the foreign investments of US companies and maintain the comfortable lifestyle enjoyed by middle-class US citizens. In 1953, the CIA helped overthrow a democratic government in Iran after its president proposed nationalizing the Iranian oil fields, which would have undercut the profits of multinational oil corporations invested in Iran and threatened higher oil prices in Europe and North America. In 1954, the CIA helped overthrow the democratically elected government in Guatemala, which had introduced land reform policies that would have redistributed large land holdings controlled by a few wealthy families to the many landless peasants for subsistence farming; doing so threatened the profit potential of the large banana plantations controlled by the rich families colluding with the US-based United Fruit Company, the major importer of bananas from Central America to the US at the time, which asked the CIA to intervene. In 1973, the CIA helped overthrow and assassinate democratically elected President Allende of Chile, a socialist who had expropriated the Chilean copper mines from US companies and nationalized this key natural resource for the benefit of the many poor of his country. In all three cases, the US subsequently backed dictatorial regimes that crushed the poor peoples of those countries for decades to come.

Jesus thus teaches his disciples to put away the insatiable "striving" after material things that drives conflicts and causes wars. "Instead, strive for [God's] kingdom, and these things will be given to you as well" (Luke 12:31). But can we trust God to protect and provide? "Do not be afraid, little flock, for it is your Father's good pleasure to give you the kingdom" (v. 32). God's salvation in Jesus, which promises us the goods of the kingdom, frees us from the fear of not enough, the fear that fuels our striving and strife. Amid the striving and strife of this world, then, comes to us a saving word from God—"Do not be afraid . . . do not worry"—to deliver us from our penchant for conflict and war. Heeding this first word of God's message, those who are receptive and responsive to God's salvation in Jesus are called to live as a sign of contradiction to the "striving of the nations." Those who have been delivered from worldly striving by the good news, and who trust God for their protection and provision, are released from the world's way of war to follow Jesus in the way of peace. This is good news!

3

HAVE FAITH

Salvation and Healing

"You of Little Faith"

Having been delivered from fear and worry by the first word of good news, we are freed to respond with all of our heart, mind, and strength to God's salvation in Jesus. We have seen how Mary, Peter, James, and John responded with whole-self commitment, submission to God's word in heart and mind that puts strength into action for the kingdom. In gospel terms, it is this active pursuit of God's word of salvation—"following Jesus"—that shows what it is to "have faith." The connection is drawn by Jesus in the passage we have just reflected upon in the previous chapter. After telling his disciples to "[c]onsider the ravens" and "[c]onsider the lilies" and assuring them that God will provide for them as well as for the birds and the flowers, Jesus chides them—"you of little faith!" (Luke 12:28). God's promise of protection and provision frees Jesus' followers *from* fear- and worry-driven striving for the things of this world; and, trusting God, Jesus' followers are freed *to* divest themselves of earthly treasure—"Sell your possessions, and give alms"—and invest their lives in God's kingdom: "Make purses for yourselves that do not wear out, an unfailing treasure in heaven" (vv. 33-34).

What is "heavenly treasure"? That which counts by God's standards, that which has weight in God's scales—deeds of justice and mercy. Being free from worldly striving for the sake of striving for God's kingdom, the disciples can now make themselves ready to actively respond to God's word: "Be dressed for action and have your lamps lit" (v. 35). Indeed, that is what Peter, James, and John had done when Jesus first called them: "they left everything and followed him" (5:11).

Notice that Jesus' chiding interjection—"you of little faith!" (12:28)—marks a transition between instruction about God's provision—"Consider the ravens . . . Consider the lilies . . . " (vv. 22-28)—and exhortation to committed action: "do not keep striving . . . do not keep worrying . . . Instead, strive for [God's] kingdom . . . Do not be afraid . . . Sell your possessions, and give alms" (vv. 29-33). This movement from fear and worry to commitment and action is *hinged upon* faith. In a sense, the readiness to respond in active trust to God's word *is* faith. Thus, to be *un*willing to divest of earthly treasure and invest in heavenly treasure—by sharing generously from one's abundance with others in need—is not only to fail to do justice and love mercy but it is to lack faith, to lack trust in God's promise to protect and provide.

"Your Faith Has Saved You"

The faith that is active trust in committed pursuit of God's salvation in Jesus is exhibited in a number of scenes in Luke's narrative. The first is the story of the healing of a paralyzed man (5:17-26). Jesus is teaching one day in a house in Galilee while Pharisees and scribes crowd around to hear what the rabbi will say. But this will be no ordinary Torah lesson, for "the power of the Lord was with him to heal" (v. 17). As he is teaching, a group of men come to the house "carrying a paralyzed man on a bed" and "trying to bring him in and lay him before Jesus" (v. 18).

Because of the crowd, however, there is no room for them to enter the house by the door. Not to be denied in their pursuit of healing for their friend, "they went up on the roof and let him down with his bed through the tiles into the middle of the crowd in front of Jesus" (v. 19). Jesus immediately recognizes their collective quest: "When he saw their faith, he said, 'Friend, your sins are forgiven you' " (v. 20). Of course, a debate ensues with the Pharisees and scribes, who charge Jesus with blasphemy for presuming the authority of God to forgive sins (v. 21). Jesus replies to them by healing the man as a sign of his authority to forgive sins: " 'But so that you may know that the Son of Man has authority on earth to forgive sins'—he said to the one who was paralyzed—'I say to you, stand up and take your bed and go to your home' " (vv. 23-24). Healed instantly, the man stands up, takes his bed, and heads for home, giving God the glory and leaving the crowd in awe of God (vv. 25-26).

The hinge in this story that links the quest of the paralyzed man and his friends and Jesus' offer of forgiveness and healing is Jesus' recognition of their faith. Notice how the text puts it: "When [Jesus] *saw* their faith . . . " (v. 20). What did Jesus see? He saw the relentless persistence of folks who would not be thwarted from bringing their friend to Jesus. The faith that Jesus saw is precisely the trust that acts in committed pursuit of God's salvation; this is the faith that receives God's forgiveness and healing in Jesus.

The next scene in which such faith is exhibited is that of the healing of the Roman centurion's slave (7:1-10). Jesus has just finished teaching the people about the way of God's kingdom and entered Capernaum (v. 1). When Jesus enters the city, the news of his coming goes out ahead of him; and when the centurion "heard about Jesus, he sent some Jewish elders to him, asking him to come and heal his slave" (v. 3). The elders of the synagogue comply with this request, for the centurion is a friend of the Jewish community in that city. So they come to Jesus to plead the centurion's cause on his behalf: "He is worthy of having you do this for him, for he loves our people, and it is he who built our synagogue for us" (vv. 4-5). Jesus responds to their quest without question and proceeds with them to the centurion's house. "[B]ut when he was not far from the house, the centurion sent friends to say to him, 'Lord, do not trouble yourself, for I am not worthy to have you come under my roof; therefore I did not presume to come to you. But only speak the word, and let my servant be healed'" (vv. 6-7).

At this point, the centurion has pursued Jesus through two different emissaries who carry two quite different messages to Jesus. The Jewish elders plead the centurion's cause on the premise of his *worthiness* to receive the gift of healing for the slave. Luke does not tell us that this centurion is a "righteous gentile" who "fears God and does right" (as was Cornelius, Acts 10:2). Instead, the elders emphasize that he has shown favor to their synagogue. It thus seems that they count the centurion worthy of Jesus' help because he favors them; and by seeking Jesus' help they are evidently looking to return the favor. The centurion himself sees his position in opposite terms, as one of *un*worthiness. He knows his position in the eyes of God; and thus his posture toward God's salvation in Jesus is not one of self-merit. Indeed, his sense of unrighteousness heightens at the approach of Jesus, such that the centurion does not see himself worthy even of prostrating before Jesus (as had Peter; Luke 5:8). Instead, the centurion sends intermediaries to plead with Jesus that he keep his distance, "for I am not worthy to have you come under my roof" (7:6). Yet, although the centurion counts himself unworthy of Jesus' favor, he recognizes the healing authority of Jesus' word: "only speak the word, and let my servant be healed" (vv. 7-8).

It is only here that Jesus responds verbally to the centurion's petitions—up to now, Jesus has not said a word. Now Jesus has a word to speak to the crowd following him: "I tell you, not even in Israel have I found such faith" (v. 9). At this reply the centurion's friends depart back to the house, where they find the slave already healed (v. 10). In all of this, the Roman centurion, in contrast with the Jewish elders, has shown faith; and it is the centurion's faith, rather than the elders' recommendation, to which Jesus has responded with a healing word. What is this faith that Jesus has found in him? The centurion's faith was simply that, upon hearing the good news about Jesus (v. 3), he actively pursued without hesitation the salvation of God in Jesus. Though knowing himself to be unworthy of Jesus' presence, he persists in quest of a word from Jesus, trusting in its healing authority. This trust-in-action is the faith that receives the saving help of God's word in Jesus.

In another scene Jesus accepts a dinner invitation to the house of Simon the Pharisee (7:36-50). After Jesus takes his place at the table, "a woman in the city, who was a sinner, having learned that he was eating at the Pharisee's house," comes and prostrates herself, weeping, at the feet of the reclining Jesus and proceeds to lovingly bathe his feet with her tears and dry them with her hair, kissing and anointing them with perfume (vv. 36-38). The scene concludes with the woman having been forgiven of her sin and sent forth by Jesus in the peace of God's salvation: "Your faith has saved you; go in peace" (v. 50). In the meanwhile, Simon has questioned to himself Jesus' judgment and wisdom: "If this man were a prophet, he would have known who and what kind of woman this is who is touching him—that she is a sinner" (v. 39). Jesus responds by telling Simon a parable of a creditor who forgives two debts—one small, the other large—and the contrasting gratitude of the forgiven debtors, the upshot of which is that "the one to whom little is forgiven, loves little" (v. 47).

Jesus uses the parable to compare the contrasting responses of the woman and his host, how she has shown him the proper attention due to a guest while Simon has neglected his duties as host (vv. 44-46). Simon, secure in his self-righteousness, confident in his worthiness to dine at table with Jesus (and even questioning Jesus' worthiness to dine with him!), shows Jesus little love. And he shows little love because he fails to recognize that he is in the same position as the woman—that he is a sinner in the presence of the one who has authority to forgive sins (cf. v. 49). She, by contrast, lavishes upon Jesus the love of one who knows her sin all too well but also knows her forgiveness by

God through Jesus. In all this, the woman says not one word. Yet by her actions, by her persistence in love, a love that breaks through the barrier of prejudice keeping "sinners" from the table, Jesus sees her faith, through which she is saved by God's grace. Again we see a faith that, upon hearing of the good news about Jesus (v. 37), acts trustingly and boldly in quest of God's forgiving salvation.

The scene in which the bleeding woman is healed presents a similar picture of faith (8:42-48). Jesus is on his way to the home of the synagogue leader, whose daughter is dying (vv. 41-42). This woman has been on a twelve-year quest to find true healing, having been exploited by many physicians who took her money but offered her no relief (v. 43). She is one among many in the crowd surrounding Jesus as he makes his way (v. 45). Now, that she suffers chronic hemorrhaging entails, according to the ritual purity laws, not only that she herself is unclean but that everything and everyone she touches is unclean as well (Lev 15:25-27). The purity laws thus erect a barrier between her and the salvation of God in Jesus—because she is "unclean" and "contaminating" of those around her, she is unworthy to approach Jesus. Not to be thwarted by legal roadblocks in her quest of healing, "She came up behind him and touched the fringe of his clothes, and immediately her hemorrhage stopped" (Luke 8:44). Jesus then questions who has touched him; and the disciples, not having seen what has happened, gesture ignorantly toward the pressing crowd (v. 45). They miss the point of the question—"Who touched me?"—which refers not just to the physical impression of one body upon another, but to the deliberateness, the purposefulness, of the contact. Jesus continues to insist, "Someone touched me; for I noticed that power had gone out from me" (v. 46). Her transgression having been exposed, the woman comes forward, trembling, and falls prostrate before Jesus, confessing before all present the reason for her transgression and the healing she had received (v. 47). Jesus then gives his approval to what she has done: "Daughter, your faith has made you well; go in peace" (v. 48). Note that Jesus uses the same Greek verb—"to save" (*sōdzō*)—as in the previous scene with the forgiven woman: "your faith has saved you" (NJB).

What faith is this, though, that Jesus has recognized in her? Luke does not tell us in this scene that Jesus has seen her faith, only that he has felt power going out of himself and heard her confession. And because Jesus announces that "your faith has made you well," her faith must have been manifest prior to her being healed, which of course precedes both his noticing her touch and hearing her confession. Now, in contrast to the other gospel accounts, both of which open a window into her motivation ("If I but touch his clothes, I will be made well"—Mark 5:28; cf. Matt 9:21), Luke's account offers us no insight into the mind of this woman. Luke thus focuses our attention upon her action—her persistence in moving through the crowd in pursuit of Jesus, her boldness in overcoming fear of social disapprobation and transcending the limits of the law in order to reach Jesus. This trust-in-action, then, is the faith through which she has received God's healing salvation in Jesus.

Faith and Counter-Faith

Finally, we come to the scene outside Jericho in which Jesus heals a blind man who is "sitting by the roadside begging" (Luke 18:35-43). To have our eyes fully opened to the significance of this blind man's saving faith, we should look to see what has just happened on the way to Jericho. Jesus is teaching the people when "a certain ruler" asks Jesus what he must do "to inherit eternal life" (18:18-25). Jesus instructs him to keep those of the ten commandments that the rabbis summed up, "love your neighbor as yourself" (v. 20; cf. 10:25-28). When the man says that he has kept all these commandments his whole life, Jesus adds "one thing lacking"—"Sell all that you own and distribute the money to the poor, and you will have treasure in heaven; then come, follow me" (v. 22). This is the same instruction that

Jesus has given earlier to his disciples (12:32-34); and it is the same condition that he lays down for the crowds: "none of you can become my disciple if you do not give up all your possessions" (14:33). Before following Jesus, each one must count the cost of discipleship (14:25-32): Am I able to trust God enough to leave my possessions so that I may give all for the kingdom? To inherit eternal life, therefore, this man must respond to Jesus' invitation to follow him and seek God's kingdom above earthly treasure. Attached to his possessions, he fails to act: "But when he heard this, he became sad; for he was very rich" (18:23).

Jesus comments, "How hard it is for those who have wealth to enter the kingdom of God!" (v. 24). Wealth, Jesus implies, impedes salvation (inheriting eternal life/entering the kingdom of God). Keeping your wealth for yourself hinders keeping the commandment of God by loving your neighbor as yourself; storing up treasure on earth thus comes at the expense of storing up treasure in heaven. Like weaponry, wealth is an attempt to secure earthly existence by worldly power. Security in wealth or weapons, however, is false security. Those who try to secure earthly life by human means, Jesus warns, will succeed only at losing life ultimately, while those who sacrifice all for the kingdom of God will be saved: "Those who try to make their life secure will lose it, but those who lose their life will keep it" (17:33). Implicitly, then, securing earthly life by wealth or weapons is *counter-faith*, a vain attempt to save oneself. As with the man in this story, when we put our trust in wealth or weapons, we miss the way of salvation.

Now we reach the outskirts of Jericho. Having witnessed the aborted discipleship of the rich ruler, we encounter one who is absolutely poor. In stark contrast to the rich ruler, this blind beggar has no earthly security and is utterly dependent upon the mercy of others. Already lacking possessions, he has nothing other than his blindness to leave behind for the kingdom of God. When he hears the crowd going by, he inquires what is happening and learns that "Jesus of Nazareth is passing by" (18:36-37). Immediately, he shouts, "Jesus, Son of David, have mercy on me!"—an outburst that provokes a command of silence from the crowd, a rebuke intended to keep him in his place "by the roadside" (vv. 38-39). Not to be silenced, he shouts all the more loudly, "Son of David, have mercy on me!" (v. 39). This brings Jesus to a halt. Jesus summons the crowd to bring the man to him; "and when he came near, he asked him, 'What do you want me to do for you?'" The man replies directly, "Lord, let me see again" (vv. 40-41). Then Jesus speaks the healing word: "Receive your sight; your faith has saved you" (v. 42).

Again we see that Jesus declares that this blind man has been saved through faith; and again we wonder what this faith is that Jesus recognizes and through which the man receives healing. Jesus heals the man upon the man's answer to his query, "What do you want me to do for you?" The man's answer, "Lord, let me see again," however, does not reveal his faith so much as lay out his petition before Jesus. The faith to which Jesus responds has thus already been evidenced, but where? What halts Jesus in his steps is the man's second, louder plea for Jesus' attention and mercy. Jesus heeds the man's cries, not because the man has called him "Son of David," a messianic title, which he uses in both pleas. Rather, Jesus recognizes the man's faith in the palpable urgency of his plea, the audible resolve of his voice straining against the stifling "Shush!" of the crowd, his indefeasible insistence of moving from periphery to center. This is his faith, this active, persistent pursuit of God's salvation in Jesus.

"I Will Arise and Go to Jesus"

In each of these stories, the faith through which our characters are saved by God's grace is made evident by action. The evidence of their faith, that which Jesus recognizes and to which he responds, is not belief but behavior. Notice again how the text puts it in our first story, when the friends bring the paralyzed man to Jesus. It doesn't say, "When Jesus heard, 'I believe,' . . ."

—it says, "When [Jesus] *saw* . . . " None of these characters in pursuit of healing and forgiveness preface their quest for God's salvation in Jesus by formulating their theological doctrine or testifying to their personal conviction. Professing a creed, or even confessing Jesus as "personal savior," would seem to be a side matter. Instead, it is their boldness and persistence in going to Jesus despite physical, social, legal, and spiritual barriers that demonstrates what it is to "have faith."

Each of these characters performs in his or her own way the words of the classic spiritual. The song issues an invitation to us "sinners" that we should "come to Jesus" who is "ready to save":

> Come, ye sinners, poor and needy,
> Weak and wounded, sick and sore;
> Jesus ready stands to save you,
> Full of pity, love, and pow'r.

The singer responds to the song's invitation with a resolve to *act*, to "arise" and "go to Jesus":

> I will arise and go to Jesus,
> He will embrace me in His arms;
> In the arms of my dear Savior,
> O there are ten thousand charms.[2]

Saving faith involves a whole-self response to the good news: "arising" to "go to Jesus" implicates one's entire existence—heart, mind, and strength—in a movement *from out of* one's unworthiness and need *toward* forgiveness and healing in the saving "embrace" of God extended through "the arms" of Jesus.

This transcending movement of faith is especially visible in the cases of the forgiven woman and the man who receives sight. The "woman of the city, who was a sinner" arises from the pit of judgment into which the Pharisees have cast her by moving the very body that is the agency of her own sin and object of others' reproach into Jesus' presence and using that body to lovingly bless Jesus, whereby she receives grace and peace. The blind "roadside beggar" arises from the ditch of social marginalization in which public sentiment keeps him put down by amplifying the very voice that is the means of his begging and the concern of his censors until it breaks into Jesus' attention, whereby he receives healing and restoration.

The faith that Jesus recognizes, the faith through which we receive salvation, is *trust-in-action*—active trust in God's promise to protect and provide and in God's power to forgive and heal, made evident in persistent pursuit of God's presence in Jesus. The faith through which we are brought near to God's salvation and are sent forth in God's peace involves a whole-self response to the good news of Jesus. And our appropriate response to God's salvation—God's protection and provision, forgiveness and healing—is to follow Jesus: "Immediately, he regained his sight and followed him, glorifying God" (18:43).

4

BEAR FRUIT

Salvation and Repentance

"The Way of the Lord"

Our movement of faith beyond fear in response to the good news of Jesus must also, if it is to reach maturity, "bear fruit." This call to "bear fruit" is front and center in the ministry and message of Jesus' forerunner, John. And the prerequisite of bearing the right fruit, John preaches, is repentance.

After "the word of God came to John," John "went into all the region around the Jordan, proclaiming a baptism of repentance for the forgiveness of sins" (Luke 3:2-3). John's message of repentance echoes the message of the prophet (3:4-6; cf. Isa 40:3-5):

> The voice of one crying out in the wilderness:
> "Prepare the way of the Lord,
>   make his paths straight.
> Every valley shall be filled,
>   and every mountain and hill shall be made low,
> and the crooked shall be made straight,
>   and the rough ways made smooth;
> and all flesh shall see the salvation of God."

The ministry of John anticipates the coming of the Lord; and the purpose of John's ministry is to prepare the people for their visitation from God. The way of salvation for the people of God is "the way of the Lord," which is none other than the way of repentance. The coming of the Lord requires radical changes—that valleys be filled, mountains be lowered, crooked become straight, and rough become smooth—in order to make ready the "straight path" of God's salvation.

John's message to the crowds that come out to his revival meetings by the river Jordan is simple: "Bear fruits worthy of repentance" (Luke 3:8). There can be no substitute for the path of repentance. Claiming one's inheritance of salvation promises through the faith of past generations without bearing the right fruit simply will not do. Those who fail to "bear fruit" put themselves in jeopardy of being severed from God's people: "Do not begin to say to yourselves, 'We have Abraham as our ancestor'; for I tell you, God is able from these stones to raise up children to Abraham. Even now the ax is lying at the root of the trees; every tree therefore that does not bear good fruit is cut down and thrown into the fire" (3:8-9). The people's repentance is the appropriate response to the good news of God's coming, the only way in which the people can ready themselves to receive God's salvation.

"A Day Acceptable to the Lord"

The message John preached—that God's restoration is conditional upon the people's repentance—was not new; it had been heard before in Israel. Following the dedication of the new temple, Solomon received a message from God in a vision. Such a grand edifice, God said, does not qualify the covenant obligations of both the people and the king to seek God and follow God's law. The temple is nice, but do not even so much as pretend that temple worship can substitute for covenant faithfulness:

ritual sacrifice cannot substitute for the people's repentance; the people must "turn from their wicked ways" to receive God's blessing (2 Chr 7:12-22).

This message was proclaimed repeatedly by the prophets. Isaiah sounds this message right from the beginning, likening Judah and Jerusalem to Sodom and Gomorrah because they had failed to be faithful to God's covenant due to iniquity and injustice. All the best sacrifice, incense, observance, and prayer by the people cannot in any way "cover" or "compensate" for the sin that the people had committed. The people's worship pleases God only insofar as the people heed "the teaching of our God," cleanse their ways of evildoing, and "learn to do good" and "seek justice" for the oppressed, orphan, and widow (Isa 1:10-17). The proper worship of God is the sacrifice of repentance, which entails not only a deliberate turning from evil but also the purposeful pursuit of righteousness and justice in the cause of the poor, weak, and vulnerable. The result of repentance will be the spiritual cleansing and social blessing of the people (vv. 18-19). But, the prophet warns, those who refuse to repent from wrong and turn toward the right will incur God's judgment (v. 20). The prophet's call to repentance thus marks a parting of ways, a divergence of futures, among the people: those who repent "shall be redeemed by justice," those who rebel "shall be destroyed altogether" (vv. 27-28).

The prophet Amos likewise proclaims that in the economy of God's salvation there is no exchange rate between sacrifice and sin that would allow the people to give God due by offering sacrifice as a substitute for righteousness and justice. Evidently, the people wanted a covenant with God that would permit them to oppress the poor, deny basic rights to the weak, pay unfair wages to laborers, exploit the debts of the needy—and then make things right with God by offering sacrifice in the temple. God accepts no such deal (Amos 5:21-24):

> I hate, I despise your festivals,
> and I take no delight in your solemn assemblies.

> Even though you offer me your burnt offerings and grain
> offerings,
> I will not accept them;
> and the offerings of well-being of your fatted animals
> I will not look upon.
> Take away from me the noise of your songs;
> I will not listen to the melody of your harps.
> But let justice roll down like waters,
> and righteousness like an ever-flowing stream.

The upshot of the prophet's message is that, far from sacrifice being acceptable as satisfaction for the people's sin, worship pleases God only insofar as the people give God due by doing right by one another. Where injustice and oppression reign, worship is falseness and infidelity: don't "mouth pious irrelevancies and sanctimonious trivialities" (as the Rev. Martin Luther King Jr. put it[3]); defend the cause of the poor!

The prophet Isaiah takes this message to its radical conclusion: not only is worship no substitute for justice, but doing justice for the poor *is* the proper worship of God. The prophet confronts a people that seeks God's ways and desires God's blessing "*as if* they were a nation that practiced righteousness" (Isa 58:2).[4] When no response from God is forthcoming, the people cry out, "Why do we fast, but you do not see?" (v. 3). The prophet's retort is sharp and pointed, exposing the people's injustice and violence (vv. 3-4):

> Look, you serve your own interest on your fast day,
> and oppress all your workers.
> Look, you fast only to quarrel and to fight
> and to strike with a wicked fist.

"Such fasting," which conceals injustice behind the mask of superficial piety and cloaks violence with the sackcloth and ashes of false humility, the prophet declares, "will not make your voice heard on high" (v. 4). The prophet then proclaims in the voice of God (vv. 5-7):

> Will you call this a fast,
> a day acceptable to the LORD?
> Is not this the fast that I choose:
> to loose the bonds of injustice,
> to undo the thongs of the yoke,
> to let the oppressed go free,
> and to break every yoke?
> Is it not to share your bread with the hungry,
> and bring the homeless poor into your house;
> when you see the naked, to cover them,
> and not to hide yourself from your own kin?

Not only is restoration conditional upon repentance, but oppression-overturning, captivity-breaking, hungry-feeding, homeless-sheltering, nakedness-covering justice *is* the piety and humility that pleases God (vv. 8-14).

Notice a common feature of the prophetic message—the *plural* character of repentance and restoration. In each case:

> the call is made to a *people*;
> the people are called to turn away from *corporate* sin;
> and the benefit of God's blessing is *social* justice and peace.

Repentance, the preparation appropriate to receiving God's salvation, is not merely an individual affair, enclosed within the secrecy of one's heart or the privacy of one's mind and exposed only to God's sight. God's prophet calls for a communal, corporate response to the good news, a response that is open to public scrutiny and witnessed by manifest effects.

This message of old is for the church of today: All of our worship—all our singing and preaching, all our prayers and offerings, all our baptismal and eucharistic rites—are nothing in God's sight, even offensive to God, *unless* the church is committed—heart, mind, and strength—to walking humbly the way of justice and mercy (Mic 6:6-8). Sacrificial offering, the prophet declares, is no substitute for covenant loyalty: "I desire steadfast love and not sacrifice, / the knowledge of God rather than burnt offerings" (Hos 6:6). Jesus, who echoes the prophets (cf. Matt 9:13; 12:7), likewise takes aim at our best piety: "But woe to you Pharisees! For you tithe mint and rue and herbs of all kinds, and neglect justice and the love of God; it is these you ought to have practiced, without neglecting the others" (Luke 11:42). If the church ignores the injustice and violence that "sell the needy for a pair of sandals" and "trample the head of the poor into the dust" (Amos 2:6-7) but sings "Glory to God" and expects Jesus to "receive our prayer," then our worship is no less than an affront to God, insult added to injury.

A long line in Christian tradition, which penetrates deeply into the heart and mind of the church, understands Jesus' death "for us" on the cross as a "substitution" in the very way that the prophets reject as contrary to God's covenant. In this way of thinking, "the blood of Jesus" is appropriated by the church as a "substitute" for our doing deeds of justice and mercy; in effect, we make an exchange with God, Jesus' sacrifice for our sins, which "makes things right" with God. This "virtual exchange" allows us to offer Jesus' sacrifice to God instead of the justice and mercy to which the prophets call us. In effect, Jesus' sacrifice becomes a divine proxy for human holiness, such that, instead of living humbly in the presence of God with deeds of justice and mercy (Mic 6:8), we simply invoke "the blood of Jesus" as "cover" for our sins while our actual lives remain unchanged.

Following the prophets, the apostle Paul rejects the idea that a covenant of faith with God can exist on such terms. Paul was aware of the danger of falling into such thinking and warns against it. Having expounded God's surpassing love for us in Christ—"But God proves his love for us in that while we were still sinners Christ died for us" (Rom 5:8)—Paul preempts the faulty reasoning that if "Christ died for us" while we were yet in our sins, then as long as we "have faith" we need not repent of our sins to enjoy God's blessing. Evidently, some in the early church were even claiming that Jesus' sacrifice created an "exchange rate" between sin and grace: we "exchange" our sins for

Christ's grace "by faith" and are thereby "made right" with God. In this way of thinking, our many sins only multiply God's grace, so that the more we sin the greater is God's grace we receive "by faith." To such claims, Paul retorts, "What then are we to say? Should we continue in sin in order that grace may abound? By no means!" (6:1-2).

Such thinking misunderstands the "for us" of Christ's death: Christ died "for us," not as a surrogate, a replacement for our righteousness, but to render us capable of righteous living. Paul sets us straight on the matter: Christ died "for us" to make holy human lives possible. Christ's death dealt decisively with sin in order to liberate us from the enslaving power of sin that, through the weakness of the flesh, works death in us. And the power of the Holy Spirit, by which we are buried and raised to life with Christ in baptism, enables us to "walk in newness of life" and thus do the works of justice and mercy that God's covenant requires (Rom 6:2-23; 8:1-17). Jesus' sacrifice does not substitute for our own sacrifice but rather demonstrates what our true worship of God should be—the offer of our very selves as a "living sacrifice, holy and acceptable to God" (12:1).

Hearing and Doing

Jesus, like John and the prophets before him, calls his followers to "bear fruit." Having chosen "the twelve" from among his disciples to be apostles (Luke 6:13-15), Jesus instructs a large gathering of his disciples and other followers in the ways of God's kingdom (vv. 20-38). His sermon concludes with two closely related teachings, one on bearing fruit and the other on obedience to God's word. Just prior to these teachings, Jesus tells a parable (vv. 39-42):

> Can a blind person guide a blind person? Will not both fall into a pit? . . . Why do you see the speck in your neighbor's eye, but do not notice the log in your own eye? . . . You hypo-

> crite, first take the log out of your own eye, and then you will see clearly to take the speck out of your neighbor's eye.

This parable on hypocrisy is effectively a call to repentance. Before we point out the sins of others (the speck in our neighbor's eye), we ought to first excise the sins in our own lives (the log in our own eye), for we tend to see in others the sins that we deny in ourselves.

Jesus follows this with a parable on bearing fruit (vv. 43-45):

> No good tree bears bad fruit, nor again does a bad tree bear good fruit; for each tree is known by its own fruit. Figs are not gathered from thorns, nor are grapes picked from a bramble bush. The good person out of the good treasure of the heart produces good, and the evil person out of evil treasure produces evil; for it is out of the abundance of the heart that the mouth speaks.

Good fruit is borne by a good tree, bad fruit by a bad tree. The tree here is the human heart, and the fruit borne is the good or evil, the justice or injustice, that is produced in word or deed. Thus, just as one knows the kind of tree by the fruit it produces, one knows the "treasure" of the human heart by the "abundance" it produces in justice or injustice. Jesus is exhorting his hearers to bear "good fruit" in the form of right words and deeds; and the parable implies that doing so requires that one look first to the condition of one's own heart. As with the parable about hypocrisy, the call to bear good fruit is effectively a call to repentance, to excise the "evil treasure" of one's heart and exchange it for "good treasure."

Jesus concludes his teaching with another parable (vv. 46-49):

> Why do you call me "Lord, Lord," and do not do what I tell you? I will show you what someone is like who comes to me, hears my words, and acts on them. That one is like a man building a house, who dug deeply and laid the foundation on

> rock; when a flood arose, the river burst against that house but could not shake it, because it had been well built. But the one who hears and does not act is like a man who built a house on the ground without a foundation. When the river burst against it, immediately it fell, and great was the ruin of that house.

This parable pictures for us the complete, threefold response to the salvation of God in Jesus: come to Jesus; hear the word of God; act on the saving word one has heard. All those in the crowd had come to Jesus and heard the word (and so, ostensibly, had taken the first two steps); and, apparently, many in the crowd had taken to calling Jesus "Lord." The parable implies, however, that simply professing Jesus as "Lord" is an incomplete response. The echoes of the prophets now resonate in our ears: going to church, listening to the homily, putting money in the offering plate, taking communion, and professing faith in Jesus are no substitute for obeying Jesus—piety without discipleship that puts into practice the teaching of Jesus is a house without foundation destined to crumble and fall. This parable of obedience completes the previous parables on hypocrisy and bearing fruit: those who come to Jesus and hear the word but do not act on Jesus' teaching and yet presume to call Jesus "Lord" are not only shaky houses, but hypocrites with logs in their eyes for all to see, bad trees whose fruit in unjust words and deeds will expose the "evil treasure" of their unrepentant hearts.

Later on, Jesus tells another familiar parable about "bearing fruit" that pictures a full response to God's word. Jesus is on an evangelistic tour through Galilee, "proclaiming and bringing the good news of the kingdom of God" (8:1). With the exhortation, "Let anyone with ears to hear listen!" Jesus tells this parable to the gathered crowd (vv. 5-8):

> A sower went out to sow his seed; and as he sowed, some fell on the path and was trampled on, and the birds of the air ate it up. Some fell on the rock; and as it grew up, it withered for

> lack of moisture. Some fell among thorns, and the thorns grew with it and choked it. Some fell into good soil, and when it grew, it produced a hundredfold.

Jesus then interprets this parable to his disciples (vv. 11-15):

> Now the parable is this: The seed is the word of God. The ones on the path are those who have heard; then the devil comes and takes away the word from their hearts, so that they may not believe and be saved. The ones on the rock are those who, when they hear the word, receive it with joy. But these have no root; they believe only for a while and in a time of testing fall away. As for what fell among the thorns, these are the ones who hear; but as they go on their way, they are choked by the cares and riches and pleasures of life, and their fruit does not mature. But as for that in the good soil, these are the ones who, when they hear the word, hold it fast in an honest and good heart, and bear fruit with patient endurance.

The parable of the sower presents a picture that contrasts varying effects of God's word (the "seed") in various hearers (types of "soil"). The basis of comparison that shows up the difference among the cases is not whether folks have heard the word—the same "seed" falls on each—but rather how each responds to the word received. Whether God's word has a full saving effect in our lives, whether we "bear fruit," depends upon our response to the good news we have received in Jesus.

In the first case, the word is snatched away by the devil to preempt God's salvation. These recipients are said to be "those who have heard" (v. 12); that is, they have heard *only*, having made no active response to the good news, such that the word fails to germinate, without effect. In the second case, the seed germinates but the young plant withers for lack of roots to reach moisture. These recipients are said to be "those who, when they hear the word, receive it with joy" (v. 13). This second group does respond to the word, receiving it "with joy," but a merely emotional response, however intense, does not provide the deep "soil" necessary for faith to form "roots." This response proves to be superficial, "they believe only for a while," such that the saving effect of God's word is stunted—the growth of faith sprouted from the word withers in the heat of trial. This group parallels those in the parable about obedience, who fail to build their lives upon Jesus' teaching and thus whose dedication dissipates under the pressure of persecution. The lesson: euphoric spirituality, without discipleship to undergird it, is at best a shallow-rooted plant, a shakily built house.

In the third case, the seed germinates, puts down roots, and begins to grow but is "choked" by "thorns" so that "their fruit does not mature." These recipients are said to hear the word and then "go on their way" (v. 14). This third group fails to "bear fruit" precisely because, having heard the word, they "go on their way." Satisfied with a one-time "conversion experience," they continue living in the same way. They don't turn from "their way" to follow Jesus in "the way of the Lord" and thus don't make the change of life that is needed if God's word is to bear fruit. The growth of faith is eventually stifled by those very things—"the cares and riches and pleasures of life"—against which Jesus warns his disciples (12:4-34). Here we realize that the parable of the sower, too, is about repentance: the full effect ("mature fruit") of God's word requires that, upon receiving it, we turn *from* the way of "worry" and "striving" after the things of this world and turn *toward* the way of God's kingdom.

In the fourth case we see a full, fruitful response to God's word. These recipients are said to not only "hear the word" but also "hold it fast in an honest and good heart, and bear fruit with patient endurance" (8:15). In Luke's gospel, Mary is the paradigm of the disciple who hears the word of God, holds it fast in a pure heart, and "bears fruit"—Jesus! This full, fruitful response has two aspects. First, these recipients of God's word "hold it fast in an honest and good heart." The reference to "an honest and good heart" recalls the parable about bearing fruit—good fruit is borne by a good tree, good deeds are the "abundance" produced from the "good treasure" of the heart from which sin has been excised. It also contrasts with the hearers in the third group. They deceive themselves because their desires remain fixed on the things of this world so that their hearts remain unchanged by God's word. Only a repentant heart can "hold fast" to God's word with honesty and goodness. Second, those responding fully to God's word "bear fruit with patient endurance." The reference to "patient endurance" contrasts with the immediate and intense but shallow and short response of the second group of hearers, in whom the sprouted word withers in the heat of trial. The "mature fruit" of salvation worked by God's word comes through patient endurance in suffering and persecution. And such patient endurance must be founded upon active trust—faith!—in God for protection and provision.

The Unfruitful Tree

Jesus, like John, explicitly links bearing fruit to repentance in a warning of judgment (13:1-9). On his way to Jerusalem, Jesus is teaching when some in the crowd give him the news that fellow Galileans have been slaughtered in the temple on order of Pilate (v. 1). Sensing that the crowd might interpret this event as a sign of God's judgment on select sinners, Jesus reminds them of those who were killed by a toppled tower in Jerusalem (v. 4) and warns all present that they are in need of repentance just as much as anyone who happens to suffer catastrophe: "do you think that they were worse offenders . . . No . . . unless you repent, you will all perish just as they did" (vv. 3, 5). Jesus then tells a parable of a barren fig tree (vv. 6-9):

> A man had a fig tree planted in his vineyard; and he came looking for fruit on it and found none. So he said to the gardener, "See here! For three years I have come looking for fruit on this fig tree, and still I find none. Cut it down! Why should it be wasting the soil?" He replied, "Sir, let it alone for one

> more year, until I dig around it and put manure on it. If it bears fruit next year, well and good; but if not, you can cut it down."

If we link together Jesus' response to the report of Pilate's slaughter in the temple ("unless you repent, you will perish") and the parable of the barren fig tree that follows ("If it bears fruit . . . well and good; but if not . . . cut it down"), we see that Jesus is repeating John's message: "Bear fruits worthy of repentance" (3:8).

In Jesus' parable, the vineyard owner who announces judgment upon the fig tree is looking for the fruit appropriate for a fig tree—figs. The prophets used the image of a vineyard as a picture of Israel, whose owner and caretaker is God (cf. Ps 80:8-18; Jer 2:21). And Isaiah uses the vineyard image to depict God bringing judgment upon an unrepentant Israel that bears the wrong fruit (Isa 5:1-7). What "fruit" is appropriate for God's "vineyard"? Justice and righteousness, the prophet proclaims (Isa 5:7):

> For the vineyard of the LORD of hosts
> is the house of Israel,
> and the people of Judah
> are his pleasant planting;
> he expected justice,
> but saw bloodshed;
> righteousness,
> but heard a cry!

Belonging to the prophetic tradition, Jesus' parable, like John's preaching, is a warning of judgment: if you do not bear fruit appropriate to repentance, if you do not keep faith with God by deeds of justice and righteousness for your neighbor, you will be uprooted from God's people and disinherited from God's promises. As with John's warning, the judgment Jesus announces is for all God's people. No one can escape from God's judgment—no one can claim a superior righteousness that will grant them a special immunity. The salvation of God's people depends upon the people's repentance: without repentance, God's people are like the tree without fruit and the house without foundation—destined for destruction.

This message—repent or perish—does not, of course, strike us as good news. It is good news, nonetheless. Jesus is showing us God's way of salvation. And unless we heed Jesus' word of warning, we will miss the way. The question for us is, "What then should we do?"

5

DO RIGHT

Salvation and Justice

"What Then Should We Do?"

John has told the crowds that have come to him to be baptized that they must do more to "[p]repare the way of the Lord" than simply invoke the name of Abraham. There is no clause in the covenant exempting Abraham's descendants from the Lord's requirement that they are "to do justice, and to love kindness, and to walk humbly with God" (Mic 6:8). Claiming a privileged ancestry—"My grandmother was a saint" or "My father helped build this parish"—cannot substitute for "bearing fruit." If God wanted only to multiply Abraham's descendants, God could "raise up children to Abraham" from the stones of the earth (Luke 3:8). The aim of the covenant, however, is fidelity, justice, righteousness, and mercy.

Hearing John's preemptory rebuke, the crowd inquires, "What then should we do?" (3:10). John replies, "Whoever has two coats must share with anyone who has none; and whoever has food must do likewise" (v. 11). The firstfruits of the people's repentance is economic redistribution—voluntary sharing by those whose material abundance exceeds their need with those whose meager possession falls short of their need. Notice that those who ask

John, "What then should we do?" are not "the rich." In Luke's gospel, "the rich" are frequently singled out for attention; but here it is simply "the crowds" that John admonishes to repentance. The call to share applies to all those having "two coats"—one more than necessary. So, *anyone* who has *more than needed* is to share with those who have less than what they need. Notice also "must"—John does not offer a suggestion but issues an imperative. Sharing one's abundance with others in need, while to be done voluntarily, is *not optional*—it is justice appropriate to repentance. Covenant justice requires that the hungry be fed, the naked clothed, the homeless sheltered, and so forth. Indifference to human need is not an option for God's people; to ignore the needs of others is to fail to be "a child of Abraham."

Economic redistribution as the firstfruits of the people's repentance is exemplified by the early church. After Peter proclaims the resurrection of Jesus and the coming of the Holy Spirit, the people in Jerusalem, convicted of complicity in Jesus' death, ask Peter the same question the crowds had asked John: "what should we do?" And Peter replies with the same message: "Repent, and be baptized every one of you in the name of Jesus Christ so that your sins may be forgiven" (Acts 2:37-38). Then "those who welcomed his message were baptized," received the teaching of the apostles, and joined the fellowship and worship of believers (vv. 41-42). The faith community, empowered and guided by the Holy Spirit, instituted a voluntary practice of economic redistribution: "All who believed were together and had all things in common; they would sell their possessions and goods and distribute the proceeds to all, as any had need" (vv. 44-45; cf. 4:32-37). This voluntary practice of economic redistribution continued beyond the church at Jerusalem through the ministry of Paul. Appealing to the example of Jesus, who became poor for our sakes so that we might obtain the riches of salvation (2 Cor 8:8-9), Paul calls the church at Corinth to contribute to the collection for the church at Jerusalem, which was experiencing hardship: "I do not mean that there should be relief for others and pressure on you, but it is a question of a fair balance between your present abundance and their need, so that their abundance may be for your need, in order that there may be a fair balance" (vv. 13-14). The implication of Paul's exhortation is that the church should institute practices of economic sharing that would maintain a "fair balance" of material goods between those having an "abundance" and those having "need."

Christian tradition retained this apostolic teaching that economic redistribution is the fruit of repentance and imperative of justice. Saint Basil, the fourth-century bishop, emphasizes this teaching in his homily on Jesus' parable in Luke's gospel about the rich man with the productive fields and overflowing barns. Instead of sharing this abundance with his needy neighbors, he builds bigger barns to store up his goods so that he might live comfortably for many years. God then judges him because he has stored up treasure for himself but has failed to be "rich toward God" (Luke 12:16-21). Basil says that this man, by keeping his abundance all for himself, fails to love his neighbor as himself—and thus fails to do justice as God's covenant requires. He then addresses the argument to all of us who have more than needed but would try to justify saving it all for ourselves:

> "But whom do I treat unjustly," you say, "by keeping what is my own?" Tell me, what is your own? What did you bring into this life? From where did you receive it? . . . The things you received in trust as a stewardship, have you not appropriated them for yourself? . . . The bread you are holding back is for the hungry, the clothes you keep put away are for the naked, the shoes that are rotting away with disuse are for those who have none, the silver you keep buried in the earth is for the needy. You are thus guilty of injustice toward as many as you might have aided, and did not.[5]

As the children of God, we are to share the goods that we would save up to secure our future comfort so that the immediate needs of the poor may be satisfied today.

Hear, then, what our forebears in faith are saying to us: Insofar as we have stored food in our pantries, unused clothing in our closets, extra space in our houses, or surplus cash in our accounts, but we do not voluntarily and generously share of our God-given abundance with those lacking necessities, then we, like the Pharisees, "neglect justice and the love of God" (11:42).

"They Do Not Know How to Do Right"

Next, the tax collectors ask, "Teacher, what should we do?" John replies, "Collect no more than the amount prescribed for you" (3:12-13). John's reply presupposes that tax collectors are guilty of collecting more than the prescribed amount. At first glance we might thus think that John has issued the innocuous injunction that every good Israelite would have known, "Obey the law." Not so. To see what injustice he's exposing, one needs to know something about the Roman provincial tax collection system in Palestine during the first century. Rome imposed upon its subjugated peoples two main taxes: the agricultural tribute, requiring one-quarter of the biennial crop produced by each landholder; and the poll tax, an annual denarius per-person tribute for the mere privilege of being a Roman subject. The Roman provincial government authorized selling the rights to collect taxes to local persons through a "tax farming" system (better for the *Pax Romana* that the subjugated people despise their own for collecting taxes). Those who won competitive bids to collect taxes for a district were the chief tax collectors (e.g., Zacchaeus), who could then subcontract with others to do the actual tax collecting as his agents (e.g., Matthew). The Roman government set the basic poll taxes and property assessments that the chief tax collector was responsible to collect and hand over, but did not strictly limit how much money could actually be collected from each household. The real levy paid by the peasants was set by the chief tax collector, who typically demanded a not inconsiderable "surcharge" on the tax and assessment (return on investment). On top of that the tax collecting agent was free to add his own "collection fee" (reward for the risk). Tax collecting was thus a rather profitable private enterprise. When the tax collecting agent came to your door backed by Roman-authorized soldiers, you had little option but to pay up if you could, and perhaps go hungry until the next harvest; or mortgage the family farm to a rich lender (who might well be in cahoots with the tax collector) and sell yourself into servitude to feed the family and repay the debt if you had to; or else get "the sword" of government (prison or worse) for your trouble if you resist paying. The only limit to the amount of tax collected was the depth of the pockets and patience of the peasants—too much taxation and they might revolt, which would bring down the wrath of Rome for upsetting the "peace." This crushing system was a *legal* means by which a privileged few, protected by the implied violence of Rome, could amass wealth and land by exploiting the weakness and vulnerability of compatriots. That is why "tax collector" was used in conjunction with "sinner" in first-century Palestinian Jewish vernacular, why organized armed peasant resistance ("Zealots") targeted tax collectors and their soldier escorts, and why the rebels who liberated Jerusalem from Roman rule in 66 CE burned the tax records in the temple treasury.

In admonishing the tax collectors to repent, John is exposing *legalized* extortion and exploitation of the poor; he is thus railing against structural injustice and systemic violence. Effectively, John is echoing the message of the prophet (Amos 3:10):

> They do not know how to do right, says the LORD,
> those who store up violence and robbery in their strongholds.

This message is pertinent for today. For now as then the law permits and protects many forms of exploitation of the poor in financial and business dealings; and now as then too many of us regard such exploitation as "business as usual." The only difference is that now the exploitation is quite often subtle and wears the face of social respectability. As the Southern black freedom movement leader Rev. C. T. Vivian once put it, "Robbery can be a piece of paper. Robbery can be the fine print. They call it 'predatory lending.' Amos called it *robbery*."[6] While some will call the practices of sub-prime lenders and pay-day lenders "business as usual," if you lost your house to the bank because you were not sophisticated enough to understand the complicated mortgage terms, or if you were caught in a cycle of debt because you could not keep up with the excessive interest on your emergency loan, you would understand why the prophet calls it nothing less than "robbery."

Now, we might still think that the tax collector's repentance is simply to stop exploiting the poor, nothing more—collect only what's due. That would overlook a key point—justice is the fruit of repentance, and justice requires restitution (cf. Lev 6:1-5; Num 5:5-8). We see such repentance in the cases of Matthew and Zacchaeus.

Matthew (Levi) is a tax collection agent. Jesus passes by Levi's tax booth and says, "Follow me" (Luke 5:27). Levi's response to Jesus' call is immediate and decisive—"And he got up, left everything, and followed him" (v. 28). Levi leaves behind his lucrative tax-collecting position, not even taking time to settle accounts. One might think his repentance is complete at this point. Not quite. "Then Levi gave a great banquet for him [Jesus] in his house; and there was a large crowd of tax collectors and others sitting at the table with them" (v. 29). The "others" at table with Jesus and Levi were "sinners." The Pharisees thus scold Jesus' disciples for dining "with tax collectors and sinners" (v. 30), to which Jesus replies, "I have come to call not the righteous but sinners to repentance" (v. 32). The calling of Matthew is about repentance first, discipleship second; he must "do justice and love mercy" before he can "walk humbly with God." Levi exhibits the fruit of justice appropriate to repentance. He abruptly ends his legal practice of economic exploitation, and then acts with generosity to make restitution out of his unjust abundance by inviting many "sinners" to a dinner party with Jesus, thus following the way of salvation in the kingdom of God (cf. 14:12-24). Levi's repentance is not simply feeling "sorry" or "sorrowful" in his heart, but transformative action—a whole-self turning from fleecing the poor to feeding the poor.

Zacchaeus "was a chief tax collector and was rich" (19:2). Being both a *chief* tax collector and *rich*, he is not only complicit in injustice but also despised by compatriots. As Jesus enters Jericho, Zacchaeus is eager to see who Jesus is but cannot see over the crowd (vv. 1, 3). So, he climbs a tree and waits for Jesus to pass (v. 4). Jesus then takes the initiative: "When Jesus came to the place, he looked up and said to him, 'Zacchaeus, hurry and come down; for I must stay at your house today'" (v. 5). By inviting himself to dine at Zacchaeus's house, Jesus effectively becomes the messenger announcing "the coming of the Lord." And Zacchaeus responds heartily: "So he hurried down and was happy to welcome him" (v. 6). Jesus' announcement and Zacchaeus's response forces open the question of who is worthy of the Lord's visitation. The crowd, being none too fond of Zacchaeus, senses the issue of propriety and brings it into the open by their grumbling: "He [Jesus] has gone to be the guest of one who is a sinner" (v. 7). Under their breath, some might even be calling Zacchaeus a "dirty bastard," an "illegitimate child" of Abraham who did not "rightly belong" to God's people. Acutely aware of his public reputation as a "sinner," Zacchaeus, now standing in Jesus' presence, confesses himself to be a sinner and offers repentance and restitution: "Look, half of my possessions, Lord, I will give to the poor; and if I have defrauded anyone of anything, I will pay back four times as much" (v. 8).

We can read Zacchaeus's repentance at two levels. At one level, that of law, Zacchaeus repents by doing justice, by giving generously of his unjust abundance to the poor and by making proper restitution to those he had exploited. At a deeper level, by divesting himself of his wealth (giving half of his goods to the poor and paying fourfold restitution is likely to leave him with little left over), Zacchaeus repents by "dying out" from under the Roman system of domination. He renounces at once both his "right to profit" as chief tax collector and the oppressive system that violently enforced his "right." Now that the justice appropriate to repentance has been done, "the way of the Lord" has been prepared and the Lord's visitation can proceed unhindered. Jesus thus says to him, "Today salvation has come to this house, because he too is a son of Abraham" (v. 9). Doing justice as the fruit of repentance is the way of salvation, the behavior appropriate to the true children of God's covenant.

Finally, the soldiers come to John, asking, "And we, what should we do?" John replies, "Do not extort money from anyone by threats or false accusation, and be satisfied with your wages" (3:14). Who are these soldiers? Not likely commissioned officers in the Roman army, but rather local recruits, perhaps serving in the temple police force under authority of the Jewish council, or serving in Herod's security forces, or "hired swords" paid by the Romans to escort tax collectors. What is the soldier's repentance? Again, as with the tax collector's repentance, we might see here simply an exhortation to end illegal practices such as extortion and false accusation. It is surely that, but, as with the tax collector's situation, there's something deeper being exposed. To get at that, I suggest beginning with the second half of John's exhortation: "be satisfied with your wages." What drives the extortion and false accusation by the soldiers is, evidently, dissatisfaction with wages; and such dissatisfaction, we might imagine, is driven by wanting more and more, the very thing about which Jesus would later warn the crowds and his disciples. These soldiers need to repent of worldly "striving," which leads them to use violence to satisfy their greed.

Yet, there is more. The violence they employ in extorting money is both implicit and systemic, as well as explicit and personal. The methods of violence John denounces are "threats" and "false accusations." At the explicit, personal level, both of these are easy to imagine, for both come at the end of a sword drawn by the "extorter" and poked into the belly or held to the neck of the "extortee." As we could imagine a mobster pointing a gun in the face of a nightclub owner to "encourage" him to pay "protection" money, we could also imagine a soldier escorting a tax collector extorting money by force of sword once the tax collector had finished extorting money by force of law. A drawn sword, however, is not necessary to extorting money; one might just as well employ implicit, systemic violence. Luke's gospel provides material for our imagination. Suppose you were a member of Herod's security forces. Having heard of Herod's paranoia and his penchant for imprisoning and beheading troublesome fellows (think John), you might extort money from someone by threatening to denounce him to Herod's advisor as a traitor. Or suppose you were a member of the temple police force. You might have heard rumors that the council is looking to prosecute and punish anyone who upsets the status quo and agitates the people (think Jesus), so you might extort money from someone by threatening to accuse him before the council as a blasphemer. In such scenarios, the extortive violence is not the explicit violence of a drawn sword, but the implicit violence of an unjust system. The repentance to which John calls these soldiers is thus not merely a renunciation of personal violence and the greed that drives it. John calls them to cease profiting by the systemic violence of abusive authority.

Now, recall that John's call for the people to repent and do justice is intended to "[p]repare the way of the Lord" (3:4). So, let's return to that earlier quotation by which the narrator sees John's ministry as a revival of the prophetic ministry (v. 5):

> Every valley shall be filled,
> and every mountain and hill shall be made low,
> and the crooked shall be made straight,
> and the rough ways made smooth.

Using a little imagination, we can see a figurative relationship between the prophetic oracle and the "fruits worthy of repentance." Preparing to receive the salvation of God requires, first, that "[e]very valley shall be filled, / and every mountain and hill shall be made low." The "valleys" to be "filled" are those lacking basic necessities, who have a deficit of material goods (the hungry, the naked, the homeless, etc.), while the "mountains" and "hills" to be "lowered" are those who have surplus goods. And the way in which the valleys are to be filled is the voluntary sharing of "stuff" from the mountains and hills to the valleys. Second, preparing the "way of the Lord" requires that "the crooked shall be made straight." The "crooked" that needs to be "straightened" is the structural injustice that allows the tax collector to legally exploit the poor. And, third, making "his paths straight" requires that "the rough ways be made smooth." The "rough ways" that need "smoothing" is the systemic violence that permits the threatening and extorting ways of the soldiers.

The prophetic oracle of Isaiah thus helps us to envision the justice appropriate to repentance in response to the good news of salvation: *economic redistribution* among God's people in order to achieve a fair balance of basic goods; an *end to legal exploitation* of the poor through unfair practices and structural injustice; and *renunciation of oppression and violence*, committed against the weak and vulnerable, and the greed and power abuse that drive them. To "[p]repare the way of the Lord" is about not only personal salvation but also structural transformation, social justice as well as individual holiness.

"Do No Wrong or Violence"

John's call to repentance was not only public, addressed to the people, but also political, addressed to the government. One task of the prophet is speaking truth to power, calling the rulers and authorities to account. Herod Antipas was evidently a frequent recipient of John's call to repentance, and he appears to have been less than appreciative of this public exposure of his sins. "So, with many other exhortations, he [John] proclaimed the good news to the people. But Herod the ruler, who had been rebuked by him because of Herodias, his brother's wife, and because of all the evil things that Herod had done, added to them all by shutting up John in prison" (3:18-20). Notice that John rebuked not only Herod's personal immorality (adultery with his brother's wife) but also "all the evil things that Herod had done"—a record of evildoing that was "added to" by imprisoning John. John's imprisonment was clearly an abuse of power by Herod, systemic violence to silence a troublemaking prophet. Thus, "all the evil things" that John exposed likely included Herod's abuses of power to eliminate threats to his authority—and perhaps more.

What might be the other "evil things" that Herod had done and which John denounced? To see what these might have been, let's recall Jeremiah's ministry during the reign of Jehoiakim, one of the last kings of Judah. John's situation is reminiscent of that of Jeremiah, who ended up imprisoned and thrown in a cistern to die for his boldness in speaking truth to power (Jer 37–38). The Lord sends Jeremiah to Jehoiakim's court to prophesy that if the king refuses to repent—to "do no wrong or violence" but "[a]ct with justice and righteousness"— his kingdom will fall (Jer 22:1-5):

> Go down to the house of the king of Judah, and speak there this word, and say: Hear the word of the LORD, O King of Judah sitting on the throne of David—you, and your servants, and your people who enter these gates. Thus says the LORD: Act with justice and righteousness, and deliver from the hand of the oppressor anyone who has been robbed. And do no wrong or violence to the alien, the orphan, and the widow, or shed innocent blood in this place. For if you will indeed obey this word, then through the gates of this house shall enter kings who sit on the throne of David, riding in chariots and on horses, they, and their servants, and their people. But if you will not heed these words, I swear by myself, says the LORD, that this house shall become a desolation.

Notice that Jeremiah addresses his warning not only to the king but also to the king's "servants" and the "people who enter these gates" (v. 2). Jeremiah denounces not only the king's evildoing but also the evildoing of the executive cabinet ministers and government bureaucracy officials as well as those who enjoy the king's patronage and the royal party members who have access to the throne. Many are complicit in and benefit from the crimes committed under the auspices of the crown.

Jeremiah then issues an indictment against Jehoiakim and his cohort, contrasting his father Josiah's just doings against his unjust ways (22:15-17):

> Did not your father . . . do justice and righteousness?
> Then it was well with him.
> He judged the cause of the poor and needy;
> then it was well. . . .
> But your eyes and heart
> are only on your dishonest gain,
> for shedding innocent blood,
> and for practicing oppression and violence.

Jeremiah cites a bill of crimes strikingly similar to those exposed by John's exhortations to the tax collectors and soldiers. First, *dishonest gain*: the rich build their expansive, lush homes on the backs of the working poor and undocumented immigrants whose labor is stolen from them by unfair yet legal practices allowing those having the bargaining advantage to dictate the lowest possible wage or even evade paying their workers (vv. 13-14). Second, *shedding innocent blood*: not likely open murder, but perhaps the lethal results of unjust laws that the powerful use to expropriate ancestral land from widows and orphans for their own mansions and flocks, leaving the vulnerable to fend for their lives without source of support (cf. Isa 10:1-2; Luke 20:47). Third, *practicing oppression and violence*: perhaps blackmailing with threats of imprisonment or death those who won't comply with injustice and those who would dare expose official crimes to public outcry, in order to coerce the weak-willed into compliance and silence the righteous opposition into complacency (cf. Jer 26).

Notice how Jeremiah links together injustice and violence (both against the poor) and identifies the king's courts as the place of exploitation and bloodshed: "do no wrong or violence to the alien, the orphan, and the widow, or shed innocent blood *in this place*" (22:3). He would also proclaim a parallel message in the temple gate: the temple has become a "den of robbers" because its authority is being abused to oppress the vulnerable and "shed innocent blood" (7:1-15; cf. Luke 19:45-46). Jeremiah is exposing structural evil within Israelite society, originating in and legitimated by its major institutions of centralized authority (the monarchy and the temple), and is calling for radical transformation toward social justice.

We might look for prophets of our own time to assist our imagination in reconstructing John's message to Herod. In many respects, the mission of the Rev. Martin Luther King Jr. drew off the prophetic heritage of Jeremiah and John. Rev. King called the nation to repentance, to turn from its ways of racism, materialism, and militarism and follow in God's path of freedom, justice, and peace. His message sounds the very same interrelated themes of economic inequity, structural exploitation, and systemic violence that we have already heard in the messages of both Jeremiah and John. Let us hear from Rev. King's final speech before the Southern Christian Leadership Conference during the last year of his life:

> I want to say to you as I move on to my conclusion, as we talk about "Where do we go from here," that we honestly face the fact that the movement must address itself to the question of restructuring the whole of American society. There are forty million poor people here. And one day we must ask the question, "Why are there forty million poor people in America?" And when you begin to ask that question, you are raising questions about the economic system, about a broader distribution of

> wealth. When you ask that question, you begin to question the capitalistic economy. And I'm simply saying that more and more, we've got to begin to ask questions about the whole society. We are called upon to help the discouraged beggars in life's marketplace. But one day we must come to see that an edifice which produces beggars needs restructuring . . .
>
> Now, when I say question the whole society, it means ultimately coming to see that the problem of racism, the problem of economic exploitation, and the problem of war are all tied together. These are the triple evils that are interrelated . . .
>
> A nation that will keep people in slavery for 244 years will "thingify" them—make them things. Therefore they will exploit them, and poor people generally, economically. And a nation that will exploit economically will have to have foreign investments and everything else, and will have to use its military might to protect them. All of these problems are tied together. What I am saying today is that we must go from the convention and say, "America, you must be born again!"[7]

Observe in this last paragraph how each social-structural-systemic sin begets the next: racism begets slavery, slavery begets economic exploitation of the domestic poor, domestic economic exploitation begets foreign economic oppression, foreign economic oppression begets military intervention, and foreign military intervention begets domestic militarism. Rev. King was thus calling for national revival through structural transformation.

Now, were John speaking such truth to Herod—as Jeremiah spoke to Jehoiakim and as Rev. King spoke to America—we could readily see why Herod went to the extent of "shutting up John in prison." John was likely preaching a message that exposed the interrelated political and spiritual evils that oppress and exploit the poor, structural injustice from which the rich and powerful profit, profits that are protected by systemic violence. And the point of John's message was likely much the same as that of Jeremiah's and King's: "do no wrong or violence"!

6

SING PRAISE

Salvation and Freedom

Whose Praise? Which Hymn?

Luke's account of Jesus' birth begins with Caesar's decree of an imperial census (2:1). Caesar, who had brought "peace and security" to the empire by defeating his rival in battle, is popularly acclaimed as "savior of the world." Because of this, Caesar is glorified as "son of a god," Augustus, the one who is worthy of highest praise, to whom obedience and reverence is now due—*kyrios*, lord, sovereign, supreme ruler (cf. Acts 25:21, 26). The poets of Rome lauded the victorious emperor as progenitor of the "golden age of peace and prosperity." Virgil penned, "This, this is he, Whom thou so oft hearest promised to thee, Augustus Caesar, Son of a god, Who shall again set up the Golden age" (*Aeneid* VI, 791–94). Horace added, "Thy age, O Caesar Augustus, Has restored to farms their plenteous crops" (*Carmina* IV, Ode XV).[8] Such imperial propaganda from prominent poets stirred up feelings of loyalty among the people and promoted the popularity of the cult of the emperor.

So the whole world obeys Caesar's command. For the peoples subject to his rule, being counted in the census for the sake of being taxed reminds them that their fates are ruled by the emperor's will, that their lives and labor belong to Caesar. For those who deify the emperor, such obedience is also an act of worship, an offering of devotion to their lord. Perhaps there were some who even sang anthems to Caesar on their way to register with the authorities, a hymn of praise lauding his wondrous acts and awesome might.

Into this chorus of the emperor's hymn breaks a word from heaven that challenges the imperial civil religion (Luke 2:14):

> Glory to God in the highest heaven,
> and on earth peace among those whom he favors!

"Glory to God!" supplants "Hail Caesar!" Doxology dethrones idolatrous ideology. In the wake of this hymn from heaven, those on earth might well have remarked, "Hark! How the heavenly anthem drowns all music but its own!" Notice that this hymn is sung by "a multitude of the heavenly host" (2:13). The "heavenly host" is, literally (in Greek), the "army of heaven." To get a sense for the imagery here, recall the ancient oracle announcing the birth of the "Prince of Peace" (Isa 9:2-7). At the advent of the Prince to reign in justice and endless peace over God's kingdom, the prophet says, "the boots of the tramping warriors / and all the garments rolled in blood / shall be burned as fuel for the fire. . . . The zeal of the LORD of hosts will do this" (vv. 5, 7). Now, at the birth of Jesus, the "heavenly host"—the Lord's own army of "zealots" for God's kingdom—announces "peace on earth." The advent of the *Prince of Peace* is hymned by the *army of heaven*—the militant arm of God's zeal is revealed as a peace choir!

Observe the implied contrast between the way of God and the ways of the world. The accession of Caesar Augustus to the imperial throne was flanked by columns of "tramping warriors" wearing "garments rolled in blood" of military victory and greeted by great throngs of people shouting "Hail Caesar!" The advent of the Messiah is attended by a small company of shepherds armed with staffs and greeted by a great throng of heaven singing "Glory to God!" The advent of the Messiah thus subverts at once *both* the official propaganda of the empire that proclaims "peace through war" *and* the revolutionary ideology of the oppressed that seeks liberation through violence. The partisans who, in the name of the "zeal of the LORD," take up the sword against Rome to force a violent end to occupation and restore independence to Israel are *not* true "zealots." The true "zealots" of the Lord are those who, like the "heavenly army," protest the empire by singing praise and practicing peace.

This authentic "zeal of the LORD" is manifest by Jesus' disciples at his entry into Jerusalem. As Jesus approaches the Mount of Olives, the disciples go ahead to prepare the way of the Lord (Luke 19:28-36). And when Jesus begins the descent, the disciples take the counterpart of the "heavenly army" by sounding an antiphon to the heavenly hymn—"the whole multitude of the disciples began to praise God joyfully with a loud voice" (vv. 37-38):

> Blessed is the king
>   who comes in the name of the Lord!
> Peace in heaven,
>   and glory in the highest heaven!

The Gloria of the angels at Jesus' birth in Bethlehem is answered by the Gloria of the disciples at Jesus' entry into Jerusalem. The song of praise from heaven to earth as the King is born in lowly estate is echoed by a song of praise from earth to heaven as the King enters the royal city. Now is revealed the true King of God's people, who comes to rule in righteousness, escorted not by a conquering army as Caesar had entered into Rome but by a multitude of the very people whom Caesar rules. When Caesar's subjects herald Jesus as the King from heaven and Prince of peace, heaven's doxology is ratified on earth and earth mirrors back heaven's peace—the imperial yoke is broken (cf. Isa 9:3-4), the real revolution is at hand!

The disciple's jubilation at Jesus' entry into Jerusalem was not the first manifestation of this authentic "zeal of the LORD" in

Luke's narrative. The first zealous response to the good news of the Messiah's advent was that of the shepherds themselves. The shepherds hear the angelic proclamation. Like Caesar's subjects who have made their way to Bethlehem to be counted in obedience to the imperial decree, they eagerly make their way to the manger in obedience to the heavenly decree. After seeing the message from heaven fulfilled in the flesh, the shepherds begin proclaiming the good news to all the people; they return to their field "glorifying and praising God for all they had heard and seen, as it had been told them" (Luke 2:20). Having seen their Savior and King, they give God thanks and praise. Perhaps this was their song too:

> Blessed is the king
>   who comes in the name of the Lord!
> Peace in heaven,
>   and glory in the highest heaven!

During the black freedom movement that brought down legal structures of racial segregation in the American South in the 1960s, the militant arm of God's zeal was embodied by the mass meetings in the churches and the peaceable columns marching in the streets of Birmingham, Selma, and Montgomery, singing, "We shall not be moved . . . We shall overcome." During the "revolution of the candles" that brought down the communist regime in East Germany in 1989, the militant arm of God's zeal was embodied in the hundred-thousand-strong peaceable throngs that gathered in prayer, song, and protest in the churches and streets of Leipzig, Dresden, and Berlin. The authentic "zeal of the Lord" that breaks the powers of domination—in the face of military occupation, legal repression, and party propaganda—is realized in the faithful disciples of Jesus who corporately embody on earth the hymn of praise and peace from heaven.

Now, Jesus' birth has been announced by the heavenly herald, who acclaims Jesus as *Christos Kyrios*—Lord Messiah, the one whose coming is "good news . . . for all the people" (2:10).

Which people? Caesar's accession to the imperial throne by victory over rivals and defeat of enemies, as we saw above, had won such acclaim from the poets of Rome. So, both Caesar and Jesus are heralded as "savior," whose coming brings "peace on earth." But the good news of Jesus' birth is a troubling word to Caesar and those whom Caesar favors. For Jesus' birth brings "peace among those whom [God] favors" (2:14). And God, as Mary has proclaimed, favors the humble over the proud who exalt themselves, the weak over the powerful who oppress others (1:50-53).

It is the peaceable coming of Jesus, not the military victories of Caesar, that is "good news . . . for all the people." It is the humble birth of a Jewish peasant, not the royal accession of a Gentile king, that signals the rebirth of the world. It is the Jewish Messiah, not the Roman emperor, through whom God will bring salvation and peace to all peoples (2:30-32; 3:6). Caesar's hymn and Christ's hymn make contending claims—Caesar has a new rival. The heavenly hymn "Peace on earth" thus anticipates not a cessation of hostilities but a conflict of kingdoms—the dominating reign of Caesar exercised through conquest and subjection, against the universal reign of God revealed in Jesus, one of Caesar's conquered subjects. For Caesar, then, this news means that warfare is not ended. The power struggle for earthly dominance by violent force must continue, a struggle to "pacify" those who now proclaim "Jesus is Lord." The good news from heaven of "peace on earth," therefore, portends a division of the people between those who receive Jesus and those who reject Jesus—and, consequently, the persecution of the loyal servants of Lord Jesus (2:34-35; 12:51-53; 21:12-19).

Singing the People Free

From the perspective of the dominating powers, doxology is a subversive song of *judgment* declaring that the empires of earth are circumscribed by the kingdom of God and subject to the lordship of Jesus. From the perspective of the oppressed, doxology is a hopeful song of *liberation* celebrating God's power to free his people from their oppressor's yoke (Isa 9:3-4). This is the posture of the songs of Zechariah and Mary.

Zechariah sings the freedom hope of a captive people (Luke 1:68-79). His song is replete with names for the manifold salvation of God: God's favor (v. 68), redemption (v. 68), salvation (vv. 69, 71, 77), mercy (v. 72), rescue (v. 74), forgiveness (v. 77), and light (v. 79). And this manifold salvation grants release from the many powers of bondage: enemies (vv. 71, 74), hatred (v. 71), fear (v. 74), sin (v. 77), darkness (v. 79), and death (v. 79). The subject of the song is not Zechariah alone, however; he sings in the voice of "we" rather than "I." The freedom hope of which he sings is not just for himself, but for "us" (vv. 69, 71, 73, 74, 78, 79), Israel (v. 68), God's people (vv. 68, 77), Abraham's children (v. 73), and the people of covenant and promise (vv. 72-73). It is thus a song of *corporate* salvation that proclaims the liberation hopes of a *people*. Although Zechariah sings of his people's liberation, the powers of bondage that he names might be interpreted as being merely personal (enemies), psychological (fear, hatred), or spiritual (sin, darkness, and death) in nature. A *people* can be held captive, however, only by powers that have political, economic, and social—as well as personal, psychological, and spiritual—forms.

Mary's song (1:46-55), like Zechariah's, is a celebration of God's salvation, both individual and corporate, both God's "favor" to his "lowly servant" Mary (v. 48) and his "mercy" to "his servant Israel" (v. 54). While celebrating God's salvation, her song too names and exposes powers of domination that hold the people captive and from which God's salvation liberates us. Notice, though, that in naming these oppressive powers, Mary does not speak of pride, power, and wealth, which might be taken to be individual vices. Rather, she speaks of "the proud," "the powerful," and "the rich," which signify powers having a structured, systemic, and social existence beyond the personal, psychological, and spiritual.

First, God "has shown strength with his arm; / he has scattered the proud in the thoughts of their hearts" (v. 51). That these "proud" are "scattered" implies that they have gathered themselves, taken on a corporate, social form. Instead of recognizing their need for God's mercy and seeking salvation in the fear of God (v. 50), these "proud" have sought salvation in their consolidated strength. Second, God "has brought down the powerful from their thrones" (v. 52). These "powerful" include the political rulers and governing authorities of this world about whom Jesus warns his disciples: "The kings of the Gentiles lord it over them; and those in authority over them are called benefactors" (22:25). They grant themselves benign titles ("savior of the world") while commanding conquering armies and controlling the conquered with repressive security police. Third, God has "sent the rich away empty" (1:53). These "rich" are not simply greedy individuals who desire accumulation of worldly goods (12:15), but also corporately organized and institutionally protected economic powers that concentrate resources in the hands of a wealthy few "who store up treasures for themselves but are not rich toward God" (12:21). The social result of this structural greed is that the poor go wanting of basic needs. Hence, "wealth" is not simply money and possessions, but the enslaving power of mammon that hinders us from doing justice for the poor and competes with God for our loyalty and devotion (16:13).

These powers sometimes operate in league. The Roman army, with the assistance of local collaborators, brutally enforced harsh provincial taxation that plundered the resources of the people and land. This oppressive system served to sustain the luxurious life of an aristocratic class in Rome and cushion the privileged life of the nation-temple establishment and chief-priestly families in Jerusalem that kept the system running smoothly. In contemporary America, the military-industrial complex robs tax money (generated by the people's labor) from social welfare programs for the poor in the name of "national security," all to enrich a few wealthy corporations that are patrons of the politicians that keep the system going. The song praising God's salvation thus proclaims liberation from such social, political, and economic powers of domination that trample the weak and deprive the poor.

Now, there is a crucial connection between the personal-psychological-spiritual powers of bondage, on the one hand, and the social-political-economic powers of domination, on the other hand; for the latter cannot hold the people captive without exploiting the former. We can observe this connection in both religious and political spheres.

The Pharisees systematically excluded the poor, blind, lame, debtors, petty offenders, prostitutes, and so on, from the synagogue. They erected legal prohibitions and cultural barriers to keep such folks from equal participation in social and economic life, considering them outcasts from God's people (cf. Luke 14–16). To justify excluding other of Abraham's descendants from God's grace, the Pharisees judged such social undesirables that could not scrupulously keep the law of Moses to be "unclean" or "sinners"—terms that justified themselves as "pure" or "righteous" under the law. Thus, the social power of the Pharisees was a function of how they used and abused "law," "righteousness," "purity," and "sin" to the advantage of themselves and to the exclusion of others. So, to proclaim "salvation to [the] people / by the forgiveness of their sins" through the Messiah (1:77), as did Zechariah, was nothing less than to proclaim the people's liberation from an exclusionary system. Hence, the claim of Jesus to forgive sins rankled the Pharisees, not only because it seemed blasphemous and circumvented the sacrificial cult in the temple, but it also undercut their control of social boundaries (5:17-26; 7:36-50). In this way, God's salvation through Jesus is both spiritual (forgiveness) and social (inclusion).

The Roman system of occupation that impoverished and dispossessed the people through burdensome taxation and repressive government could not operate without both the assistance of local collaborators to "grease the system" and the credible threat of massive use of lethal force to quell any and all resistance to Roman dominance. The use of collaborators—not only tax collectors, but also aristocratic families and political parties—created local enmities that effectively set the subjugated people over against themselves. And the threat of lethal force—by torture, prison, and crucifixion—operated on the fear of death to keep the people "pacified." Thus, to proclaim salvation through rescue from enemies, freedom from fear, and "light to those who sit in darkness and in the shadow of death" (1:71, 74, 79), as did Zechariah, cut to the heart of the people's hope for liberation from oppression under foreign rule and compatriot collaboration. Hence, the seemingly innocuous exhortation to "love your enemies" (6:27-31) implicitly counseled resistance as well as righteousness: turning tax collectors into friends (5:27-32; 19:1-10), calling Zealots to be disciples of the way of peace (6:12-16), and reconciling these mortal enemies in the common cause of God's kingdom subverts Rome's desire to rule by dividing the conquered against themselves. In this way, God's salvation through Jesus is both personal (reconciliation) and political (resistance).

Freedom from personal-psychological-spiritual powers of bondage and freedom from social-political-economic powers of domination, therefore, are really two dimensions of the same liberation. Noticing this allows us to see that the earthy freedom songs of Mary and Zechariah and the heavenly praise surrounding the eternal throne, the song of peace from the heavenly choir and its earthly antiphon by God's people, all belong to a single cantata of salvation.

Shaking the Foundations

At the inauguration of his ministry, Jesus announced that he was anointed by the Spirit of the Lord in order to "proclaim release to the captives" (4:18). As we have seen, many in Jesus' day were captive to powers of bondage—including disease, demons, and debt. The songs of Mary and Zechariah are "trumpets of freedom" proclaiming good news of release. And the ministry of Jesus brought to many people liberation from these powers, including a woman who had been physically crippled by spiritual bondage for eighteen years (13:10-17).

Perhaps most acutely captive to domination were all those, Jews and Gentiles, languishing in the darkness of Roman prisons, waiting for death, hoping for miraculous release. For Roman subjects, Roman prisons were pits of no return. The reference in Zechariah's song to "those who sit in darkness and in the shadow of death" (1:79) reflects the reality of thousands of Jews confined in the prison dungeons by the Roman authority or sentenced to serve out their lives laboring in the depths of mines or in the holds of ships. This, perhaps, is why Zechariah's song proclaims that "the dawn from on high will break upon us, / to give light" to these prisoners of darkness (1:78-79), why Jesus links the proclamation of "release to the captives" with "recovery of sight to the blind" (4:18).

Every empire—whether Pharaoh's or Solomon's or Nebuchadnezzar's or Caesar's—relies upon domination and slavery to generate economic prosperity and build up military prowess (cf. 1 Kgs 4–5; 9–10). And every dominating power seeks to pacify resistance and maintain security through an imprisonment system. The Soviet Union maintained a vast "gulag archipelago" to silence opposition and punish "enemies of the state," into which anyone suspected of disloyalty could disappear for life. And in the major cities of the "republics" occupied by the Soviet Union, the KGB operated prisons for detaining, interrogating, torturing, and executing political prisoners that dared defy the "Supreme Soviet."

That imperial power would seek to "secure the peace" through a dominating system of imprisonment should not surprise us who today live within the world's most powerful nation. To fight its global "war on terror," the United States sought to dominate its enemies by setting up a network of secret prisons into which thousands detained in Afghanistan, Pakistan, Iraq, the

US, and other places disappeared beyond the reach of legal accountability and public scrutiny. Many in these secret prisons were not only innocent of any offense but were subjected to humiliating and brutalizing conditions and torture treatment. Moreover, in order to "secure the domestic tranquility" the US has pursued a policy of mass incarceration, exponentially expanding its own prison system in recent decades—to the point of currently imprisoning some two million men and women. Those imprisoned are disproportionately racial minorities, poor, undereducated, drug-addicted, or mentally ill; and the incarcerated are often subjected to brutalizing and dehumanizing conditions (e.g., prisoner-on-prisoner rape and other dominating violence is rampant but tacitly accepted in US prisons).

This domination system of domestic imprisonment also imprisons the general public, which is enslaved to its ever-increasing demands. The burgeoning prison population, occupying ever-more-crowded and aging prisons, is largely the result of ever-more-stringent sentencing laws written by politicians preaching ever-harsher "get tough on crime" messages of retribution. Instead of being invested into education, health care, job training, or public infrastructure, ever more tax money, paid by the people's labor, disappears into the prisons along with the prisoners. Indeed, in many small towns and poor cities unable to attract genuine economic development, prisons are sold to the taxpayers as solutions to high unemployment rates and low tax bases—prosperity for the majority is promoted by prison for the minority.

We seek "peace" by oppressing the weak; we ensure "security" by brutalizing the broken; we promote "prosperity" by exiling the sinner. In the face of this domination system, the servant of salvation cries out (Isa 61:1-2; cf. Luke 4:18-19):

> The spirit of the Lord GOD is upon me,
> because the LORD has anointed me;
> he has sent me to bring good news to the oppressed,
> to bind up the brokenhearted,

to proclaim liberty to the captives,
and release to the prisoners;
to proclaim the year of the LORD's favor.

The herald of God's kingdom announces the good news to all those who are dominated and oppressed, broken and crushed, brutalized and dehumanized, captured and exiled by the imprisonment system—"Freedom!"

Liberation from the chains of imprisonment and slavery is a recurring theme among the poets and prophets of Israel, who protest against imperial domination. Rooted in and shaped by the people's historical experience of slavery in Egypt and exile in Babylon, the poet's vision of the Lord's salvation often depicts prisoners being freed and the condemned being saved (Pss 68:6; 79:11; 102:20; 146:7). Breaking iron bars and shattering prison gates are powerful images that depict the liberating activity of God on behalf of those captive to powers of domination (Isa 43:14), even those who are guilty of lawbreaking (Ps 107:10-16). And the prophet explicitly links release of prisoners with both the call of "the servant of the LORD" to the mission of justice and the time of "the LORD's favor" or "day of salvation" (Isa 42:1-7, 22; 49:8-11; 61:1-4). The poets and prophets sound a common message: God, the almighty maker of heaven and earth who keeps faith by doing justice for the poor and oppressed, wills liberation from imprisonment, the breaking asunder of bonds and bars that hold people in light-diminishing, life-defeating captivity. This God of creation and covenant thus commissions his chosen servant—called to "faithfully bring forth justice" and given as a "light to the nations"—"to bring out the prisoners from the dungeon, / from the prison those who sit in darkness" (Isa 42:3, 6-7).

The overall thrust of the prophetic message is this: imprisonment counteracts and contradicts the very freedom characteristic of God's original creative work and declared purpose for humanity, freedom that God seeks to restore through saving acts that redeem humanity from slavery and exile and establish a faith community to live in God-ordained liberty. God's gracious redeeming power seeks again and again to overthrow every power of imprisonment, to rescue humanity from all forms of bondage, so that we may give thanks and praise to God (Pss 107:15; 102:21-22; Isa 42:8; 49:13; 61:3).

Given the extent to which Luke appropriates the stories of exodus from slavery and restoration from exile to narrate the salvation revealed and realized in Jesus the Messiah, we should not be surprised to find Luke making the release of prisoners a prominent theme in his story. This is especially so regarding the stories of the early church, in which miraculous release from prison chains signals the presence and power of the Holy Spirit in the fellowship of believers (Acts 4:1-31; 5:12-42; 12:1-19). Each of the episodes of prisoners being released is closely associated with the apostle's preaching of the gospel, the prayers of the people, and the work of the Holy Spirit. In the episode of Paul and Silas in Philippi, Luke tells a remarkable story of God's Spirit breaking the power of imperial imprisonment. Like the other episodes, this liberation of prisoners is closely associated with preaching, prayer, and praise. But this story expands the scope of God's salvation to include Gentiles as well as Jews.

In the middle of the night, as they await judgment in their jail cell, Paul and Silas, prisoners in chains, "were praying and singing hymns to God" (Acts 16:25). Philippi was a Roman colony in a Greek province, so we may surmise that their fellow prisoners were Gentiles who had never before heard the good news of salvation in Jesus. Paul and Silas pray and sing out of trust in the God of Abraham and Jesus for salvation from the rulers of the darkness of this world. Yet in these petitions and praises, their fellow prisoners hear their own freedom cry: "Paul and Silas were praying and singing hymns to God, and the prisoners were listening to them" (v. 25). Perhaps this is their song (Ps 146:2-3, 5, 7):

> I will praise the LORD as long as I live;
>   I will sing praises to my God all my life long.

> Do not put your trust in princes,
> in mortals, in whom there is no help. . . .
> Happy are those whose help is the God of Jacob,
> whose hope is in the LORD their God . . .
> who executes justice for the oppressed . . .
> The LORD sets the prisoners free . . .

As they lift their bodies against the chains and their voices to heaven, the power of heaven descends to break their chains of bondage. And not just theirs but the chains of everyone listening are broken, the chains of all who find hope in the freedom song of God's salvation. "Suddenly there was an earthquake, so violent that the foundations of the prison were shaken; and immediately all the doors were opened and everyone's chains were unfastened" (Acts 16:26).

The good news of God's salvation sets free not only the Jews, Paul and Silas, but also their Gentile fellow prisoners. God's salvation from imperial imprisonment is a light breaking in upon all "those who sit in darkness and in the shadow of death" (Luke 1:79). The freedom promised by God to the people of Abraham and fulfilled in Jesus is a promise extended to those in every nation who are oppressed, a gift offered to all peoples who strain beneath the yoke of imperial bondage. The irrepressible hymn that glorifies God is the universal freedom song.

Notice: "the foundations of the prison were shaken . . . " The power of God, channeled through the prayers and praises of Paul and Silas, not only breaks the chains of bondage, but shakes the very foundations of the system that keeps the prisoners in chains. The hymn of praise that glorifies God not only breaks the chains of the prisoners, but breaks the power of the prison to hold them in bondage—it breaks the power of imprisonment. Chains unfastened can be refastened; prisoners unchained can be chained again. But unchained prisoners cannot be chained again if the prison foundations to which their chains must be fastened have been destroyed. Unfastening chains frees prisoners; shaking the foundations of the prison undermines the power of the prison. Paul and Silas realize this, as evidently do their fellow prisoners who have been likewise freed from their chains. They all remain in the prison of their own free choice despite the fact that "all the doors were opened." What holds them there is not fear of the imprisonment system, but rather faith in a God who can free them from the system that imprisons them, the same faith and the same God of which they had sung.

Even if they are chained again (which indeed would happen to Paul in other cities), Paul and Silas are *already* freed by faith in God in advance of whatever persecution they might suffer at the hand of their imperial enemies. Their song of praise announces that they have been liberated from the power of the prison—*in advance* of the forceful shaking of the prison that loosens their chains and opens the doors. Paul would later demonstrate this freedom to be under arrest "for the sake of the hope of Israel" (Acts 28:20), by electing to stand trial and bear witness to the gospel before Caesar in Rome rather than insist on being released on account of his innocence (Acts 25). The saving power of the gospel liberates Paul to remain freely in chains as a "prisoner of Jesus Christ" (Eph 3:1) in order to proclaim the good news of salvation to the very heart of the empire.

Having been freed by the gospel from the power of the prison, Paul and Silas, trusting God for salvation, are not only free to remain in prison but also are freed from taking vengeance upon their enemy, the Roman jailer. Only moments before, this jailer had represented the imperial imprisonment system and earlier had collaborated in the torture of Paul and Silas (Acts 16:22-24). The earthquake catches the sleeping jailer off guard. Paul and Silas could have seized the jailer's sword and killed him; or they could have escaped during the confusion and left the jailer to his fate in Rome's hands. Even had they not killed the jailer outright, by escaping from prison they would have jeopardized the jailer's life. It was this same freedom by the gospel of Jesus that, fifteen centuries later, enabled the hunted Anabaptist leader Dirk Willems to turn back and rescue his pursuer from icy waters rather than run for his life, even though in doing so he risked arrest, imprisonment, torture, and death at the stake.[9] By their costly choices, Paul, Silas, and Dirk testify that seeking one's own physical security and liberty while risking the life of another person, even one's enemy and persecutor, is a freedom unworthy of the gospel of Jesus.

Instead of taking advantage of the situation for themselves, Paul and Silas take this opportunity to seek the jailer's salvation. For they recognize that the jailer, though he executes Rome's power to imprison, is not himself free; his life, too, is held captive by the imperial threat of death. "When the jailer woke up and saw the prison doors wide open, he drew his sword and was about to kill himself," afraid that he would be executed for having lost his prisoners (v. 27; cf. Acts 12:18-19). Freed by God through prayer and praise, Paul and Silas, proclaiming good news of salvation in the name of Jesus, now offer the jailer the benefits of the freedom God has granted. And, by trusting God, the jailer, too, is freed from fear (vv. 28-32):

> But Paul shouted in a loud voice, "Do not harm yourself, for we are all here." The jailer called for lights, and rushing in, he fell down trembling before Paul and Silas. Then he brought them outside and said, "Sirs, what must I do to be saved?" They answered, "Believe on the Lord Jesus, and you will be saved, you and your household." They spoke the word of the Lord to him and to all who were in his house.

And in their shared freedom through faith from fear of empire, these former enemies—oppressor and oppressed, torturer and tortured—are reconciled together in Christ (vv. 33-34):

> At the same hour of the night he took them and washed their wounds; then he and his entire family were baptized without delay. He brought them up into the house and set food before them; and he and his entire household rejoiced that he had become a believer in God.

The testimonies of Rev. King and Rev. Woods are the same as that of Paul and Silas. Those who sing the song of freedom, to protest their oppression by hateful human hands and express their hope for liberation by God's saving arm, are *already* freed *in advance* of being locked up in the jail. This freedom of God's people, secured by faith in anticipation of the coming kingdom revolution to reverse injustice and restore freedom, releases the people from fear so that they might go to the jail singing their freedom all the way. Because the people are freed from fear to go to jail *voluntarily*, the dominating power of the prison is dismantled and disarmed: the jail no longer holds the people captive, and its jailers are captivated by the people's song!

Doxology—the song of praise that glorifies God—proclaims the saving movement of God's freedom in history. It is song that both hails the freedom of a God that is sovereign over history and summons the saving power of God's sovereign freedom into history. Indeed, in a real sense—as articulated by Zechariah and Mary, as evidenced by Paul and Silas, as expressed by Rev. King and Rev. Woods—singing doxology both anticipates and realizes God's saving freedom. To sing of hope for God's freedom to break into history is to perform one's freedom in God: doxology both announces and enacts, here and now, God's ultimate liberation to come.

This song of doxology not only announces the good news of God's salvation, but carries the freedom movement of God's coming. The song by which the people sing God's freedom is, in a real sense, the path of the people's freedom as they stride toward the justice and peace of God's kingdom. As Rev. King put it, "In a sense, songs are the *soul* of a movement."[13] This spirit—that the freedom song of the oppressed not only points toward the freedom that is the source of hope and objective of struggle but *is* the way of freedom—is expressed in the South African freedom song "Lizobuya," by Mbongeni Ngema:

> The liberation must be carried always through the music—
> The liberation, the liberation, through the music . . .

> Oh, through the song, through the music.
> We shall dance to the rhythms of the freedom . . .
> Oh freedom.[14]

The movement of the freedom singer dancing to "the rhythms of the freedom" concretely embodies the freedom movement of God's salvation through Jesus. The God-given freedom of voice and body, enacted in the song and "carried . . . through the music," is sign and reality, prefiguration and incarnation—sacrament—of salvation.

7

GO IN PEACE

Salvation and Mission

In the foregoing chapters, we have reflected on what it means to receive and respond to the good news of Jesus so that God's saving purpose may come to fullness in and through us. Let us recall briefly what we have heard:

"Fear not"—the good news we receive from God's messenger delivers us from fear and striving to trust in God's saving faithfulness.

"Have faith"—the good news invites us to faith, to passionately and humbly pursue the healing power and forgiving mercy of God and commit oneself trustingly into the care of God.

"Bear fruit"—the good news calls us to repent from sin and injustice, both personal and social, and turn one's whole self toward God's kingdom.

"Do right"—the good news demands deeds of justice and mercy for the poor and oppressed and words of judgment and warning for political systems of violence and economic structures of exploitation.

"Sing praise"—the good news liberates us *from* bondage to fear and sin, setting us free *to* sing the praise of God's peace and the hope of God's people, in contrast to the propaganda of the empire and in protest against the powers of domination.

We reflect now on one further, essential aspect of our response to the gospel—the calling of the church to receive the commission of the Messiah and be sent forth with the gift of God's peace, in word and deed, even for enemies of God's kingdom. Our response to the good news of salvation remains incomplete so long as we remain isolated individuals. A full response to the gospel incorporates us into the community of faith, which commissions us to "go in peace."

The Lord's Servant

Having been led into the temple by the Holy Spirit, and having taken the infant Jesus into his arms as he was presented by his parents, Simeon sings, "Lord, you now have set your servant free to go in peace as you have promised" (Luke 2:29, Book of Common Prayer). Go in peace to do what? It is typically commented that Simeon, having seen the Messiah and sung his song, leaves the scene, exits the stage, and, satisfied at seeing the Savior, retires from ministry to enjoy "his peaceful rest." I suggest otherwise. Having been restored to freedom by the appearing of the Messiah, he is dismissed from the temple with a sign of peace to go forth on a mission from God. Simeon here is not sent off to die quietly at the old folks home; instead, God is sending him out to raise a ruckus about the gospel!

Simeon "was righteous and devout, looking forward to the consolation of Israel" (2:25). He is one of the "faithful remnant" of Israel, waiting expectantly for the visitation of God's salvation. Like the prophet Anna, Simeon hoped the Messiah would bring "the redemption of Jerusalem" (v. 38). That Simeon is "righteous and devout" indicates that he has committed his life to doing God's will—the Lord's word is his command. His posture toward God is thus the same as Mary's: "Here am I, the servant of the Lord; let it be with me according to your word" (1:38). Simeon, like Mary, is one of those who are blessed of God for having surrendered to divine lordship in the service of God's kingdom: "Blessed . . . are those who hear the word of God and obey it!" (11:28). This posture of the faithful servant surrendered to the divine purpose is perfectly fulfilled in Jesus: "Father, if you are willing, remove this cup from me; yet, not my will but yours be done" (22:42). Simeon, then, like Mary and Jesus, is a servant of the Lord.

And "the Holy Spirit rested on him" (2:25). Simeon is not only a faithful servant of the Lord, but one upon whom God has sent the Holy Spirit. Simeon is thus also a prophet, one who awaits a word, a sign, a revelation from heaven, a message for the people. He had been given a sign: "It had been revealed to him by the Holy Spirit that he would not see death before he had seen the Lord's Messiah" (v. 26). What a sign! The Holy Spirit promises Simeon that the Lord's Messiah would appear in his own lifetime! Simeon is not, however, waiting in Jerusalem to die. That Simeon "would not see death" before the Messiah had appeared does not mean that Simeon is to die upon seeing the Messiah: the Holy Spirit promised, not that Simeon would die, but that the Messiah would come! Simeon is thus hoping to see the Messiah, the promised Savior who would be Israel's true righteousness and everlasting peace. Simeon, once he has seen the Messiah with his own eyes, will not then have nothing more to live for. Instead, having seen the Messiah, the purpose of his devotion will have been confirmed.

Far from waiting to see the Messiah so that he can go to his "rest in peace," Simeon, the servant of the Lord, is waiting expectantly for the word of his Master, ready to do his will. The coming of the Lord's Messiah brings freedom to the servant Simeon: "Lord, you now have set your servant free to go in peace as you have promised" (2:29, Book of Common Prayer). What is this freedom that the Lord is granting to Simeon? Notice that the servant has not been set free *from* his Master—he remains "your servant." This freedom is thus not a release from the Lord's service. Rather, the servant is being released from his hope-full waiting precisely in order to perform his Master's service. The servant is being released from *waiting* so that he might be free for *service*. The Lord is thus sending Simeon forth on a mission of service—to proclaim the "good news" of the Messiah as "revelation to the nations" and "glory to Israel." We might even imagine that Simeon left the temple with Anna, who "began . . . to speak about the child" (v. 38), to go on an evangelistic tour of Jerusalem with the message, "The Messiah is come!"

A Peace Church

Tradition commonly says that the church of Jesus the Messiah was born at Pentecost. At that time, the Holy Spirit was poured out on the disciples of Jesus gathered at the house in Jerusalem as promised by Jesus (Acts 2:1-4; cf. Luke 24:49; Acts 1:8). The gift of the Spirit issues forth in the proclamation of the powerful deeds of God in many languages and the inspired preaching of Peter that Jesus, though crucified, has been vindicated as Lord and Messiah because God has raised him from the dead (Acts 2:5-36). A great ingathering of believers from all nations followed as thousands of Jewish pilgrims repented and were converted to faith in Jesus as Lord and Messiah (vv. 37-40). These new converts were then incorporated by baptism into the body of believers at Jerusalem, which was formed by the Spirit into a community of worship, fellowship, and sharing (vv. 41-47).

This is all true, of course. I would like to suggest, however, that the church is born with Jesus and *re*born (born again!) at Pentecost. If we see what is happening in Luke 1–2, we find there a primal church, the sprouted kernel from which the later growth took its root. As many commentators have observed, the overall narrative movement of Luke 1–2 is parallel to that in Acts 2. The story, which opens by locating itself in history ("In the days of King Herod of Judea"), begins to overcome the inertia of history with the messenger's appearance to Zechariah, announcing the birth of John, and Elizabeth's conceiving a child according to the angel's word (Luke 1:8-25). The story then gains momentum when the Holy Spirit comes upon Mary and Jesus is conceived in her by the power of God as promised by the angel (vv. 26-38). This Holy Spirit-powered movement picks up speed when Elizabeth is "filled with the Holy Spirit" at Mary's visit, and Mary sings an inspired song about God's salvation (vv. 39-56). The movement carries forward when, following John's birth, Zechariah is "filled with the Holy Spirit" and sings a prophetic song about the coming Savior (vv. 57-79). Then, following the annunciation of Jesus' birth by the heavenly messenger (2:1-14), the shepherds join in this movement of the Spirit by praising God and proclaiming the good news about Jesus (vv. 15-20). In time, a gathered community that practices worship and evangelism, table fellowship and economic sharing takes shape around Jesus during his ministry (5:29-32; 8:1-3).

Reflecting upon the nativity story, we can characterize the primal church as follows: those who receive the gospel message, trusting in God's word and hoping in God's promise, gather around the living presence of God's salvation in Jesus, to give God thanks and praise for the gift of Jesus and to go out and proclaim the good news of salvation and peace. We can see this primal church take root and grow in three particular episodes within the nativity narrative: Mary's visit to Elizabeth, the gathering of the shepherds at the manger, and the convergence of Simeon and Anna upon the Holy Family in the temple. To see this development, I suggest that we interpret these episodes through the prism of worship and liturgy.

Mary and Elizabeth are both pregnant when Mary, having learned during the angel's annunciation that God had blessed her cousin also with a son, visits Elizabeth (1:39ff.). At the meeting of these two faithful women, the first gathering in the living presence of the nascent Jesus is initiated by Mary, who greets Elizabeth and thereby calls her into Jesus' presence (v. 40). In response to Mary's call to worship, John responds by leaping for joy in Elizabeth's womb (v. 41). The Holy Spirit then comes upon Elizabeth, who continues the worship by shouting for joy and pronouncing a blessing for both Mary and the child ("fruit") in her womb (vv. 41-42). Elizabeth follows this with a confession of faith by recognizing that her Lord has visited her through the child in Mary's womb (vv. 43-44). She follows this by adding yet another blessing to Mary's blessedness (v. 45). Mary brings the worship to a climax with a hymn of praise that exalts God and celebrates his saving acts of mercy and justice (vv. 46-55).

At the birth of Jesus (2:6ff.), the membership of this primal church is extended beyond the Holy Family to include the poor and lowly, the shepherds "living in the fields" (v. 8). This time the call to worship comes from "the angel of the Lord," who "stood before them" to preside over the liturgy (v. 9). The heavenly messenger preaches a homily of "good news of great joy for all the people" (vv. 10-11) and then gives the shepherds a sign so that they might go and continue to worship in the presence of the Savior whose birth has been announced (v. 12). The heavenly choir then follows the sermon with the doxology and the sign of peace (vv. 13-14). The faithful shepherds, eager to see the angel's word fulfilled in human flesh, hurriedly follow the preacher's directions and join the family worship service, Mary and Joseph gathered around Jesus in the manger, that is already underway (vv. 15-16). After seeing their Savior, the shepherds then testify to the faithfulness of God, making "known what had been told them about this child" (v. 17); and the gathered faithful respond with amazement at the shepherds' testimony while Mary keeps silent vigil (vv. 18-19). The worship service concludes as the shepherds process forth, giving God glory and praise for the salvation and peace they had heard and seen (v. 20).

At Jesus' presentation in the temple (2:22ff.), the circle of the faithful gathered around Jesus expands again to include the oppressed and persecuted, those who are "looking forward to the consolation of Israel . . . for the redemption of Jerusalem" (vv. 25, 38). On this occasion, the call to worship comes from the Holy Spirit, who guides "righteous and devout" Simeon into the temple courts and into Jesus' presence (vv. 25-27). Upon seeing God's salvation revealed in human flesh for all people,

Simeon takes Jesus into his arms and sings a song to celebrate the universal vision of God's salvation (vv. 28-32). Mary and Joseph watch and listen in amazement (v. 33). After blessing Mary and Joseph, Simeon utters a prophetic oracle concerning the child and his mother (vv. 34-35). Anna, committed totally to worship in the temple, now enters into the worship service and breaks forth with a song of praise to God; then she "began to speak about the child," preaching a sermon about Jesus to the people gathered in the temple (vv. 36-38).

Observe three aspects of this primal church. First, the primal church is essentially a peace church, for it is conceived alongside and centered upon Jesus, who is God's gift of "peace on earth." Second, in this primal church we see several gifts of the Holy Spirit at work, especially prophecy and preaching. And all that are gifted by the Holy Spirit—women and men, old and young (even in the womb!), lay and learned, humble and devoted—have opportunity to offer something in worship to their Lord: blessing, testimony, singing, dancing, preaching, and prayer. Third, this primal church is on the social margins. Among the first to receive the good news of salvation and gather around God's gift in Jesus are the poor and lowly, the oppressed and persecuted. The primal peace church of Jesus the Messiah takes root among those who already recognize that their only hope for salvation is God.

As Luke's narrative of Jesus' nativity is carried forward by three worship scenes that bring a primal church into being, so also does Luke's narrative of Jesus close with three worship scenes that again focus our attention on a peace church taking shape. These three resurrection scenes in Luke 24—the women at the tomb, the disciples on the road to Emmaus, and the disciples gathered in Jerusalem—depict faithful and hopeful witnesses gathering around Jesus in a fellowship of peace and then going forth to proclaim good news and praise God. The chief, and crucial, difference between the three scenes of the nativity church and the three scenes of the resurrection church is that each of the latter contains significant eucharistic imagery. The death and resurrection of Jesus the Messiah effectively fills out the "body and blood" substance of the worship of the peace church.

In the first resurrection church scene, Mary Magdalene, Joanna, Mary the mother of James, and the other "women who had come with him [Jesus] from Galilee" (23:55; 24:10; cf. 8:1-3) come to the tomb at dawn on the first day of the week to show their devotion by anointing Jesus' body (24:1). It is a burial service they have come to perform. To their amazement, they found the stone rolled away and no body present (vv. 2-3). Two heavenly messengers suddenly appear beside them and deliver a short homily on the absence of the burial body of Jesus: "Why do you look for the living among the dead? He is not here, but has risen" (vv. 4-5). Jesus' dead-and-buried body is not to be their focal point; they are to seek out the risen-and-living Jesus! The messenger's homily thus calls the women to worship the living God—and to recognize the living God present in the risen Jesus. The messengers continue with their homily, reminding the women of Jesus' own words to them in Galilee that presaged what they now witness (vv. 6-7). "Then they remembered his words" (v. 8). This is the eucharistic moment, when remembering the words of Jesus and recognizing the presence—or the living absence!—of the risen Jesus converge. Caught up by the preaching of the word, the women go forth from the would-be burial service and testify to the good news of resurrection to the apostles and the other disciples, much to their amazement and disbelief (vv. 9-12).

The next resurrection church scene takes place later that day (24:13ff.). Two disciples are walking from Jerusalem to Emmaus, discussing what had happened in Jerusalem, including the incredible testimony of the women to the resurrection (vv. 13-14). While on their way, "Jesus himself came near and went with them, but their eyes were kept from recognizing him" (vv. 15-16). It is Jesus himself who initiates this worship service, even though the two disciples are unaware that they are being drawn into a worship encounter with the risen Messiah. Jesus inquires regarding what they had been discussing, and this question evokes a confession: they believe that Jesus was a prophet of God, that he was tried and crucified, and that they have heard the women's report of the empty tomb and the angels' message that Jesus was alive (vv. 17-24). They also confess the disappointment of their hope in Jesus as the Messiah: "But we had hoped that he was the one to redeem Israel" (v. 21). Their confession of lost hope in Jesus as the Messiah on account of his crucifixion precedes their confession of the empty tomb. The two are intimately linked: acknowledging an empty tomb falls short of believing in a risen Messiah; and unless they can believe in a risen Messiah, they can have no hope in a crucified Messiah. Thus, just as the women were transformed by the angels' revelation of the risen Messiah, which enabled them to testify to the resurrection, so, too, must these disciples be transformed by the real presence of Jesus so that they may also go forth to confess that Jesus is the crucified-and-risen Messiah.

To prepare them for transformation, Jesus delivers a rather lengthy sermon to explain the death and resurrection of the Messiah within the scope of the redemptive purpose of God: "beginning with Moses and all the prophets, he interpreted to them the things about himself in all the scriptures" (vv. 25-27). Despite all that preaching by the Preacher himself, they still did not recognize the risen Messiah. Nonetheless, they sensed an incompleteness, that this long sermon pointed to something more that lay beyond their grasp. So, as they neared Emmaus, they invited Jesus to share table fellowship with them (vv. 28-29). It is there, in this fellowship of peace at the table with Jesus, that the real presence of the risen Messiah, which had until then transcended their sight, is revealed to their eyes: "When he [Jesus] was at the table with them, he took bread, blessed and broke it, and gave it to them. Then their eyes were opened, and they recognized him; and he vanished from their sight" (vv. 30-31). This is the eucharistic moment, the convergence of word and flesh, made visible in the sign of bread blessed, broken, and shared. Then they realized that even as Jesus preached to them along the way they had been in the real presence of the risen

Messiah: "Were not our hearts burning within us while he was talking to us on the road, while he was opening the scriptures to us?" (v. 32). Immediately, they rise from the eucharistic table and go forth from worship to proclaim to the disciples in Jerusalem the good news of the risen Jesus who "had been made known to them in the breaking of the bread" (vv. 33-35).

While the disciples are gathered together, the third resurrection church scene begins. Again, it is Jesus who initiates and presides over this worship: "Jesus himself stood among them and said to them, 'Peace be with you'" (24:36). Having greeted the disciples with a word of peace, Jesus, sensing their fear, provides them with signs of his living-bodily reality: they are in the real presence of the risen Messiah. By showing them his hands and feet, inviting them to touch his "flesh and bones," and by eating a piece of fish, Jesus gives them not only evidence of his resurrection but also assurance that God is faithful, that God has vindicated his Messiah, that the word of God proclaimed by Jesus has indeed been fulfilled (vv. 37-44). This is the eucharistic moment where word and flesh converge—the fulfillment of God's word revealed through the real presence of the risen Jesus. Within this fellowship of peace, Jesus preaches a homily to explain all of this to them: "he opened their minds to understand the scriptures" (v. 45). Following the sermon, Jesus repeats the message and mission of the disciples—they are to preach the death and resurrection of the Messiah, and proclaim repentance and forgiveness of sins in the name of the Messiah to all nations: "You are witnesses of these things" (vv. 46-48). Jesus then promises the disciples "power from on high" to guide and sustain them in their mission and leads them out from Jerusalem, where he blesses them before withdrawing from their presence (vv. 49-51). After the liturgy concludes, the disciples return to Jerusalem, where they bless God in the temple (vv. 52-53). Thus, the liturgy that begins in the peace of the Messiah issues forth in thanksgiving and praise to God.

We see, then, that as the resurrection church takes shape around the risen Messiah in anticipation of the outpouring of the Holy Spirit at Pentecost, God's gift of peace in Jesus remains at the heart of the church. In the culminating liturgy of his ministry, Jesus proclaims, by homiletic word and eucharistic sign, that the good news of God's salvation has been fulfilled through his life, death, and resurrection. God's peace thus remains in the church eucharistically, through the convergence of word and flesh made visible in the bread that is blessed, broken, and shared as an incarnate sign of the real presence of the risen Jesus among God's faithful. And it is the continuing presence of God's peace that the church is to proclaim and share through *its* real presence in the world: the church is called to be a corporate, incarnate, visible sign of God's peace living and present in the world, a sign of the reality and nearness of God's kingdom.

To the Nations

This is a peace church with a purpose. Insofar as the church gathers around Jesus, whose birth is "good news . . . for all the people" (2:10) and who himself is "a light for revelation to the Gentiles" (2:32), those who receive this good news are commissioned to "go in peace" from worship to spread the light of Jesus and gather in from the nations all those who would believe the good news of salvation and peace. The church is to testify to Jesus, calling all peoples to repentance and reconciliation in the name of Jesus, so that "all flesh shall see the salvation of God" (3:6). After his resurrection, Jesus communicates this mission to the apostles, "that repentance and forgiveness of sins is to be proclaimed in his name to all nations, beginning from Jerusalem" (24:47). He again, prior to his ascension, commends this mission "to the ends of the earth" to the apostles along with the promise of the Holy Spirit (Acts 1:8).

This mission "to the nations" is presaged at the beginning of Jesus' ministry when in the synagogue at Nazareth he interprets "the year of the Lord's favor" (Luke 4:16-30). By way of comment on his reading from the prophet Isaiah, Jesus reminds the people of past episodes in which powerful signs of God's grace were shown to Gentiles by Elijah and Elisha (vv. 26-27). "When they heard this, all in the synagogue were filled with rage" (v. 28). The message they wanted to hear from Jesus, who had just proclaimed the fulfillment of "the year of the Lord's favor," is that God was going to bless *them* with great deeds of justice and mercy. Indeed, the songs of Mary and Zechariah, which prophesy that God is about to bring justice and freedom to his people, might seem to warrant their expectations. The folks of Jesus' hometown, however, were expecting "peace for us"—an exclusive peace with God that permitted them to continue harboring enmity and displaying hostility toward other nations. Their misguided expectation was founded upon the mistaken belief that God had specially graced them among all nations: God's blessing belonged to them, not to the Gentiles. Such misunderstanding of God's grace and peace is not unlike the sensibility of many Christians in the United States, who sing "God bless America" and "America, America, God shed his grace on thee" all the while making war with enemy nations. In the majority mind of "Christian America," God's grace to "us" and the nation's war with "them" are fully compatible. Not so, says the prophet. So the people of Jesus' own country reject God's message—that "the year of the Lord's favor" includes the gracious favoring of foreign nations with God's peace—and so reject God's messenger. Jesus had spoken truly: no prophet who preaches that God's peace is for all nations, that no one nation exclusively enjoys God's favor, is acceptable in his home country (v. 24).

Now, Jesus himself actually extends signs of grace and peace to Gentiles, as had Elijah and Elisha, by healing the Roman centurion's servant (7:2-10) and the Samaritan leper (17:11-19). Moreover, Jesus commends the faith and gratitude of such "foreigners" in contrast to those in Israel who took God's blessing for granted. Jesus thus proclaims that authentic faith in the good news of God's salvation transcends natural loyalties and national divisions. Even the foreign oppressors and historical enemies of God's people can be saved and welcomed into God's peaceable kingdom!

This supranational mission of reconciliation expands dramatically after Pentecost when the gift of the Holy Spirit is poured out on the God-fearing Roman centurion Cornelius and the other Gentiles gathered in his house (Acts 10). It is here that Peter first proclaims in full the good news of salvation and peace to all peoples without distinction: "the message [God] sent to the people of Israel, preaching peace by Jesus Christ—he is Lord of all" means "that God shows no partiality, but in every nation anyone who fears him and does what is right is acceptable to him" (10:34-36). The message of peace that Jesus preached is an invitation to the peoples of all nations to be reconciled to God. This message of salvation to all peoples on equal terms is then sanctioned by the church at the Jerusalem council through its decision to not impose Jewish legal requirements and ritual distinctions (specifically, the food laws and circumcision) upon the Gentile believers (Acts 15). The church thereby proclaimed that salvation (even for Israel) is a matter of grace, God's gift apart from merit or distinction. The God-fearing people of all nations who trust Jesus and "do right" are acceptable to God: "we believe that we will be saved through the grace of the Lord Jesus, just as they will" (15:11).

This peace mission "to the nations" had its precedent in the mission that God commended to the Jewish exiles in Babylon through the prophet Jeremiah. Jerusalem and its temple, the center of Israel's national identity and religious life, had been destroyed and the people and their leaders had been taken captive by a foreign power whose subjects worshiped false gods. Israel-in-exile questioned its very existence as God's people: How are we to be God's people in a strange land? This question took the form of national lament (Ps 137:1):

> By the rivers of Babylon—
> there we sat down and there we wept
> when we remembered Zion.

In the anguish and sorrow and humiliation of exile, corporate lament understandably turned the imagination toward vengeance upon their oppressor (vv. 8-9):

> O daughter Babylon, you devastator!
> Happy shall they be who pay you back
> what you have done to us!
> Happy shall they be who take your little ones
> and dash them against the rock!

In conquering and destroying Jerusalem and the temple, the Babylonian invaders had "killed their [Israelite] youths with the sword in the house of their sanctuary, and had no compassion on young man or young woman, the aged or the feeble" (2 Chr 36:17). The captive and exiled people imagined vengeance; God's prophet, however, counseled reconciliation. How are we to praise God by the lush rivers of Babylon, the people asked, when the ruins of Jerusalem are soaked in the blood of our children? By seeking the peace of your enemy, God answered!

Jeremiah, who remained among the ruins of Jerusalem, communicated this surprising, even perplexing, message in a letter (Jer 29:4-7):

> Thus says the LORD of hosts, the God of Israel, to all the exiles whom I have sent into exile from Jerusalem to Babylon: Build houses and live in them; plant gardens and eat what they produce. Take wives and have sons and daughters; take wives for your sons, and give your daughters in marriage, that they may bear sons and daughters; multiply there, and do not decrease. But seek the welfare [*shalom*] of the city where I have sent you into exile, and pray to the LORD on its behalf, for in its welfare [*shalom*] you will find your welfare.

Exile and captivity, near-total disaster for God's people, is transformed by God into a peace mission by and through God's people to the nations. This mission is twofold. First, the prophet tells them, instead of dealing death and destruction upon Babylonian children in vengeance for the slaughter of your children, build a life-giving community by bringing forth a new generation of children. In this way, you can build up a faithful community that passes on the teachings of God to the next generation, even among an idolatrous people. It is this faithful community that brought forth Daniel and his fellows, who, although having risen to positions of authority in the Babylonian empire, withstood threats of death from the king in order to remain faithful to God rather than worshiping the king or ceasing to pray. By their faith, not only do these young men bear witness to "the ways of the Lord" before the Babylonian people but the imperial authorities, impressed by their faith and God's protection, offer praise to God (cf. Dan 3:1-30; 6:1-28). Second, the prophet goes on, once you have built this life-giving, faith-filled community, do not keep its peace and prosperity (*shalom*) for yourselves but share with the people of Babylon; for ultimately, their well being is your well-being—when your enemy has peace, you will have peace. This peace mission can begin simply by sharing the produce of the gardens you have planted with your Babylonian neighbors and inviting into the houses you have built the hungry and homeless wandering the streets of Babylon.

The city of Israel's exile and captivity has thus become the center of a new peace mission to the nations. God's people are to carry out this mission by teaching the nations "the ways of the Lord," first through the living faith of their community and second by seeking peace for their enemies. The purpose of this peace mission is that the peoples of the nations, having learned from God's people the way of God's salvation, might receive peace in the name of the Lord and thus find a place in the midst of God's people (Jer 12:14-16). God's people are to build up a visible community of life and peace as a light to the nations so that the peoples of the nations might also come to be built up in the midst of the faith community founded upon "the ways of the Lord." Then, when both Israel and the nations have been reconciled to one another and with God, the peace of Israel and the peace of the nations might be one (Isa 2:4).

How, then, is the peace mission of the church, in its dispersion among "the nations," to proceed? Let's return to Luke's narrative to get a glimpse of the early missionary activity of the Jesus movement. When Jesus commissions the Twelve with "power and authority over all demons and to cure diseases," they are sent by him "to proclaim the kingdom of God and to heal" (Luke 9:1-2). After receiving their instructions, the Twelve "departed and went through the villages, bringing the good news and curing diseases everywhere" (v. 6). Again, when Jesus commissions the seventy to go on "ahead of him," everything that they are instructed to do is framed by proclaiming the good news of God's kingdom of peace: "Whatever house you enter, first say, 'Peace to this house!'…cure the sick who are there, and say to them, 'The kingdom of God has come near to you'" (10:5, 9).

After Jesus' death and resurrection, this kingdom mission is renewed by Jesus' teaching of the apostles "about the kingdom of God" and is empowered by the Holy Spirit (Acts 1:3-8). As the early church mission spreads beyond Jerusalem into Samaria, the leading edge of the mission is still the proclamation of the good news of God's kingdom (8:12; cf. 8:4-5, 25, 35, 40). And as Paul takes the apostolic witness to the risen Lord and Savior "to the ends of the earth," proclaiming the good news of God's kingdom remained at the heart of his mission, even as far as Rome (19:8; 20:25; 28:23; cf. 14:7, 15, 21; 17:7). Indeed, the Acts of the Apostles concludes with Paul "proclaiming the kingdom of God and teaching about the Lord Jesus Christ with all boldness and without hindrance" (28:31).

The good news of God's kingdom in Jesus thus sets the missional horizon and agenda for his followers: our mission is oriented by the advent of God's kingdom in Jesus' ministry. The historical revelation of God's reign of peace in Jesus authorizes and authenticates the church's mission. No other kingdom, and no other peace, sets the agenda for the mission of God's Messiah and so also of God's people.

Notice the holistic character of the kingdom mission authorized by Jesus: God's kingdom is to be proclaimed in *word* and *deed*: "cure the sick . . . and say to them, 'The kingdom of God has come near to you'" (Luke 10:9). Jesus commissions his followers to take up the very same mission on which he himself has been commissioned by God and empowered by the Holy Spirit—preaching and healing (cf. 4:14-44; 7:22; 9:11). Each is incomplete without the other: healing (deed) is the sign that the preaching (word) is a true message of God; and preaching (word) explains the significance of the sign of healing (deed). Word explicates sign, and sign fulfills word; word without deed is empty of power; and deed without word is empty of meaning. It is by *both* the healing sign *and* the proclaimed word that the people know that God's kingdom has come near. This holistic mission continues in the early church. Peter's preaching and healing are complementary, not contradictory or competitive. The healing of the man in the temple gate, and the healed man's praise of God, motivates Peter's preaching of the good news; and the good news about Jesus explains the healing as a visible sign of resurrection power (Acts 3; 4:8-12). Word (preaching) complementing deed (healing) is evident also in the ministries of Stephen (6:8-10), Philip (8:5-8), and Paul and Barnabas, through whom the Lord "testified to the word of his grace by granting signs and wonders to be done through them" (14:3; cf. 14:8-18). The church's mission, therefore, must avoid separating word from deed by an artificial division between "evangelism" and "social action."

Now, Jesus commissions his followers knowing that the message they bring, and the Messiah they represent, will provoke a divided response, both inviting reception and inciting rejection (Luke 9:4-5; 10:8-11). Not everyone will welcome or believe the good news that the Lord of the kingdom is coming. Indeed, rejection, not reception, marks the major transition and turning points in Jesus' ministry. Rejection had marked his inaugural preaching of God's kingdom at his hometown synagogue (4:16-30); rejection would also mark his coming into Jerusalem (19:41-48). And at the midpoint of his ministry, when he turns from Galilee to journey toward Jerusalem, Jesus' mission encounters resistance and rejection at the outset from the Samaritans: "they did not receive him, because his face was set toward Jerusalem" (9:51-56). With this experience fresh in mind, he tells the seventy frankly, "See, I am sending you out like lambs into the midst of wolves" (10:3). Having just encountered rejection by the Samaritans, and then having had to rebuke his own disciples for their less-than-peaceable desire "to command fire to come down from heaven and consume them" (9:54-55), Jesus is quite realistic about the actual effect of his messianic mission. Whether the "lambs" he is sending out ("lambs" that would call upon God to destroy their enemies!) will live at peace with the "wolves," as the prophet envisioned (Isa 11:6), is an open question at this point.

It is evident that the mission of Jesus—and thus the mission of those he sends out in his name, with his power and authority—does not bring peace to all the earth as a matter of course: God's peaceable kingdom inaugurated through the Messiah meets real resistance; and this resistance produces conflict issuing in violent rejection. God's peaceable kingdom, while present in Jesus, is thus only partially fulfilled through the messianic mission: "on earth peace for those [God] favors" (Luke 2:14, NJB). God's favor rests on those who hospitably receive the Messiah's emissaries and their peace message: "Whatever house you enter, first say, 'Peace to this house!' And if anyone is there who shares in peace, your peace will rest on that person; but if not, it will return to you" (10:5-6). In the "houses of peace" that welcome the Messiah's emissaries, the prophetic vision is indeed fulfilled—the wolf lives with the lamb! But those who reject the Messiah's emissaries and their peace message risk judgment, for to reject the peace of the kingdom is to reject the One who sent the Messiah (10:10-16). Jesus thus tells his disciples after they have returned from their mission, "Do you think that I have come to bring peace to the earth? No, I tell you, but rather division!" (12:51). Tragically, while Jesus comes to reconcile hostile parties, God's kingdom meets human resistance that engenders enmity between those who receive God's peace by welcoming Jesus and those who invite God's judgment by rejecting Jesus.

Anticipating resistance and rejection, the question facing Jesus as he commissions his followers is this: How should the disciples prepare for meeting hostility in the mission? What is to be their contingency plan? Naturally, if one were anticipating hostility, one would take proper precaution from a defensive posture—carry some form of protection (if not a weapon, then at least a staff to beat off an aggressor) as well as extra provisions (food, clothes, and money) in case no one will offer shelter. The imperial armies of Assyria, Babylon, Persia, Greece, and Rome, when marching through enemy territory, would take just such precautionary measures, of course, and were prepared to plunder their enemy if necessary for protection and provision. Jesus will have none of this, for the warring ways of the nations is counter to the peaceable mission of God's kingdom. Contrary to both natural impulse and imperial practice, Jesus exhorts his disciples not to armed defense but rather to humble trust: Jesus sends his followers in vulnerable dependence on the hospitality of strangers. In sending the Twelve, Jesus instructs, "Take nothing for your journey, no staff, nor bag, nor bread, nor money—not even an extra tunic. Whatever house you enter, stay there, and leave from there" (9:3-4). Likewise, when sending the seventy, Jesus instructs, "Carry no purse, no bag, no sandals; and greet no one on the road. . . . Remain in the same house, eating and drinking whatever they provide, for the laborer deserves to be paid . . . eat what is set before you" (10:4, 7-8). Even in the face of hostility, the kingdom mission proceeds, first and last, on trust, ultimate dependence upon God's gracious protection and provision, grace manifest in the stranger's gift of hospitality.

Jesus thus sends his followers on a mission of peace in much the same way that Jeremiah commissioned Israel-in-exile to be emissaries of peace in Babylon. Jeremiah exhorted the exiles, "Work for the good [*shalom*] of the city to which I have exiled you . . . since on its welfare [*shalom*] yours depends" (Jer 29:7, NJB). Jesus' instruction to the disciples he sends ahead of him parallels Jeremiah's instruction to the exiles: "Whatever house you enter, first say, 'Peace to this house!' . . . cure the sick who are there" (Luke 10:5-9). Just as the Jewish exiles were to seek the peace and prosperity (*shalom*) of the foreign cities to which they had been carried off into captivity, so also are Jesus' followers sent on the kingdom mission of pronouncing peace and working well-being for the strangers in whose homes they are lodged.

Moreover, the Jewish exiles in Babylon were completely vulnerable to their foreign neighbors, without any defense against the hostility of their enemies—except trust in God. They were also dependent for their well-being upon the prosperity and health of the cities in which they were held captive: if the Babylonian people suffered the ravages of famine or war or disease, the Jewish exiles would suffer the same, perhaps even more so. Thus, the notion that their own welfare (*shalom*) was inextricably bound up with the welfare of their Babylonian neighbors was not simply a pious idea, but the concrete reality of their situation. For Israel-in-exile, seeking the peace and prosperity of their enemy was not irrelevant idealism, but quite sensible realism. Similarly, the welfare of Jesus' followers sent on mission depends entirely on the generosity, prosperity, and health of those strangers who welcome them in peace. Jesus sends his disciples on their mission much as captives are taken away into exile—wearing only the shirts on their backs and the sandals on their feet, taking nothing with them except each other (9:3; 10:4). Like captives in exile, they are vulnerable to the hostility of "the other" and yet dependent upon the generosity of "the other" for shelter and food. There is only one way for such a mission to possibly succeed—by seeking the peace of "the other," trusting in God's grace. Thus, the mission on which Jesus sends his disciples is inseparable from seeking the well-being of one's enemy—proclaiming God's kingdom and pursuing peace are one and the same mission.

The apostolic mission after Pentecost continues in a similar way. The apostle's inspired preaching of "God's deeds of power" in many languages, and Peter's preaching of the crucified and risen Jesus, provokes a divided response among the crowd—some jeer, many repent (Acts 2:1-41). In this case, it is the apostolic community that hospitably receives those who hear the good news and respond with repentance, rather than the other way around: "those who welcomed his message were baptized, and that day about three thousand persons were added" to the fellowship of believers (v. 41). The preaching of the good news, and the faithful response of many, creates a visible community that is devoted to the worship and praise of God, the teaching and hearing of God's word, and fellowship and economic sharing among believers (vv. 42, 44-47). The apostolic mission of the early church soon encounters stiff resistance and open hostility from the authorities (Acts 4:1-22). Despite resistance and hostility, the apostolic mission is sustained by the faith community gathered in prayer and praise; and the community is itself empowered by the Holy Spirit to bold witness in word and deed (vv. 23-37). In the midst of threatening hostility, then, the faith community of worship and fellowship—in which the good news of Jesus is preached, the grace of God is celebrated, and the power of the Holy Spirit is present—comprises the heart of the church's peace mission.

For Today

When preaching his inaugural sermon, Jesus "unrolled the scroll and found the place where it was written, 'The Spirit of the Lord is upon me, because he has anointed me . . . to proclaim the year of the Lord's favor.' . . . Then he began to say to them, '*Today* this scripture has been fulfilled in your hearing'" (Luke 4:17-21). When announcing that the repentant Zacchaeus has shown himself to be a member of God's people, Jesus says, "*Today* salvation has come to this house" (19:9). And when pardoning the repentant criminal crucified beside him, Jesus says, "Truly I tell you, *today* you will be with me in paradise" (23:43). Jesus proclaims repeatedly throughout his ministry that the salvation and peace of God's kingdom has been revealed and is being realized in and through himself—in the present. With the advent of Jesus the Savior and the ascension of Jesus as Lord, our time has become the nascent time of God's kingdom. The time of God's salvation and peace is—today!

This concerns what theologians call eschatology. And it bears upon a crucial question for the church: *Which* peace is the church to proclaim and seek, and by what means? The church need not look elsewhere to support or join a peace movement. That God's kingdom has been inaugurated through Jesus means that the church *already* participates in the *original* peace movement—God's peace movement. Between the times of Jesus' ascension and return, the salvation and peace of God's kingdom is still being realized in the present through the church, the earthly body of the risen Jesus enlivened by the Holy Spirit. There is thus an integral connection between ethics and eschatology: the church is called to live even now the peaceable way of God's coming kingdom, for the peace that is to be when Jesus returns to reign is already becoming reality within the church. Saint Irenaeus expressed it this way in the second century: the prophet's vision of "swords into ploughshares" and "the wolf with the lamb," which is to be fulfilled for the whole world at Jesus' return, "has already happened" among the fellowship of believers, who have learned the way of Jesus and thus no longer learn the ways of war (Isa 2:2-4; 11:1-9).[15]

The gospel proclaims that Jesus Christ—by his life and ministry, death and resurrection—inaugurates a new order in world history: the kingdom of God. And the outpouring of the Holy Spirit is both the sign that this new order has begun in the church and the power by which this new order is made possible. In the dawning light of this new reality, Paul teaches the church to walk a way of holy nonconformity to the fallen pattern of the present age. Paul teaches that it is only "by the renewing of [our] minds" that we can properly discern what it is to live according to God's will: "Do not be conformed to this world, but be transformed . . . *so that* you may discern what is the will of God—what is good and acceptable and perfect" (Rom 12:2). We do not know how to live rightly until we discern God's will with a *new mind*, a mind remade by the Holy Spirit according to the pattern of Jesus Christ. The divine pattern to which we are to be conformed has been revealed to us by the righteous life and faithful death of Jesus; and the reality of that pattern is presently available to us in the church through the victoriously risen and heavenly ascended Jesus. Indeed, the apostle rebukes us, to continue living according to the fallen pattern of the present age—the way of the "old self" rather than the "new self"—is "not the way you learned Christ" (Eph 4:17-24).

Now, many Christians who call themselves "realists" will say that the peaceable way of God's kingdom is impossible in history and hence irrelevant to the church "in the meantime" until Jesus' return. In a still fallen world, where sin holds sway over human nature, they say, seeking peace and loving enemies is just not "realistic." The peaceable way of God's kingdom is thus possible and imperative for Christians only in a future time and far-off world, once evil has been finally defeated. For now, in this "real" world, Christians should follow an ethic that reckons their responsibility according to what is possible as judged by the best of human abilities. Unable to surpass the self-interest and moral weakness that afflict fallen human nature, the best we can do as Christians in a sinful world is to follow the highest of human standards. Christians should thus aim, not for the peace of God's kingdom, but for a lesser yet achievable goal—the "realistic" peace of a stability of order maintained by a balance of power. And given the reality of evil in this world, it may prove necessary to kill our enemies to establish and preserve this "realistic" peace.

This "realist" view effectively eliminates the essential tension between the commencement and fulfillment, the nascency and maturity, of God's kingdom that is distinctive of biblical timekeeping. The "realist" view places God's salvation and peace, along with the ethical imperatives of God's kingdom, "beyond history." The saving peace of God's kingdom, according to the "realist," remains elusively out of reach and out of sight for us, concealed on "the other side" of the veil of time and tears. "Christian realism," which locates the realization of God's kingdom entirely on the "far . . . not yet" side of biblical timekeeping, is thus insensitive to the biblical sensibility that God's kingdom is "*near* . . . yet far," "*already* . . . but not yet (fully)."

Rev. Gilbert Washington, pastor of St. Paul-Bethel Missionary Baptist Church in South Bend, Indiana, once characterized biblical eschatology this way: at the same time that we are moving toward God's kingdom, God's kingdom is moving toward us. This twofold movement—our looking and reaching for God's kingdom (the kingdom is "far . . . not yet") and God's kingdom coming to meet us (the kingdom is "near . . . already")—is evident in the gospel story. Jesus calls us to both "*enter* the kingdom of God" through repentance and "*receive* the kingdom of God" as a gift (Luke 18:15-25): we seek to enter what is *yet far*, and we receive what is *already near*. Indeed, Jesus instructs his disciples, "Truly I tell you, whoever does not *receive* the kingdom of God as a little child will never *enter* it" (v. 17). We cannot seek to enter God's kingdom through repentance unless we recognize that God's kingdom is near at hand, ready to be received as a gift. If we do not acknowledge that God's kingdom is coming to meet us and is *even now* ready to be received by us (as the gospel proclaims), and if instead we regard God's kingdom as remaining always "beyond history" (as the "realist" claims), then we will fail to recognize God's kingdom when it meets us and so miss our opportunity to enter it.

That is precisely the tragedy that Jesus names as he enters Jerusalem. God's kingdom has come near in Jesus and some of the people are ready to receive the good news and enter the Messiah's reign of peace. But judgment eventually falls upon Jerusalem because the nation-temple establishment is so intent on saving the status quo that they reject the Lord of the kingdom and thus fail to recognize the peace of God: "If you, even you, had only recognized on this day the things that make for peace! But now they are hidden from your eyes . . . because you did not recognize the time of your visitation from God" (19:41-44). The "realists" of Jerusalem—Herodians, Sadducees, and aristocratic families that control the Jewish council and collaborate with the Roman occupation—seek to preserve religious traditions and national institutions by way of a balance of power that maintains a stability of order. And they are willing to manipulate the system to have their enemies killed if necessary to save this "realistic" peace (cf. John 11:47-50; 18:12–19:16). But their "realism" presages the destruction, not the peace, of Jerusalem (Luke 19:43-44).

The teaching of the apostles contrasts with the view of the "realists." The apostles' teaching recognizes the reality of evil still at work in this world, but only as the remnant structure and waning spirit of the old age that is passing away. At the same time, it confesses the even greater power of God that is present in the church and active in the world. It confesses, in particular, the real power of the Holy Spirit, which enables the followers of Jesus to walk in new life, a life of holy nonconformity to the fallen pattern of the present age, the life of the kingdom to come (cf. Rom 8:1-17; Eph 1:19-21; 2:1-10; 3:16-19; 6:10-13). Moreover, the apostles' teaching concedes that, insofar as God's kingdom does not come with the overwhelming force of imperial conquest, and because it meets unbelieving resistance and violent rejection, God's kingdom remains incomplete in history. And insofar as God's kingdom is *not yet* fully realized, we are still waiting for the final redemption of our world (cf. Rom 8:18-25). Nonetheless, this expectant waiting for God's kingdom to be fully realized is pregnant with possibility, for history is not closed but remains open to the sudden and subversive advent of the freedom, justice, and peace of God as revealed through Jesus (cf. 1 Thess 5:1-3). As the church, trusting in the nascent reality of God's kingdom *already* begun in Jesus, our calling and task is to live in the light of this possibility—to both pray in anticipation of and act in accord with "your kingdom come" (Luke 10:2).

German theologian Christian Wolf testifies to this distinctive sensibility of biblical eschatology—the tension between "today" and "tomorrow," between present reality and future fulfillment. In the wake of the peaceful revolution in East Germany in 1989, in which the Protestant church played a crucial role through its ministry of prayer, peace, and presence, Professor Wolf reflected on the relationship between oppressive past, present freedom, and coming kingdom:

> In the Bible "future" has two meanings. On the one hand is the "grammatical future," that which proceeds from the present though human planning and organizing. The other is the Advent of God, which will take place not as a result of our planning. We do not have any control over it, but we can open ourselves to it in active anticipation.
>
> God has come to us in a surprising way and given us a new Germany . . . This end [of communism] has come more quickly than we thought. It came upon us as a harbinger of God's gracious future.[16]

The surprising, in-breaking act of God, which ends the old reign of oppression and opens a new era of freedom, is a gracious sign by which God's future is made *really present*—a hope-filled promise of the coming kingdom. God's liberating act releases us from the repressive grip of the historical past and so frees us in hopeful faith to see and to seek God's kingdom to come. In this way, our time becomes God's time—today becomes the day of salvation (cf. Rom 13:11-14; 2 Cor 6:2).

The narrative of Luke's gospel reveals the eschatology of God's salvation. The biblical story does not speak of salvation that eventually comes only once "all is said and done." Rather, it reveals a salvation that is awaited and received, anticipated and tasted, hoped for by us and offered by God—before our eyes, in our time. None of the figures in this story await the end of history, the cessation of all things human, the disappearing of this world. What they await is the "visitation" of God's salvation, the sudden in-breaking of God's liberating justice, here and now. The implicit eschatology of this faith story is not the expectation of "the end of time," the passing away of all temporal things, or the destruction of the world. Instead, this expectant hope is looking for the advent of the time of God's salvation—"the year of the Lord's favor."

This is especially clear when Jesus is presented in the temple. Simeon is the first to recognize the appearance of God's salvation. He recognizes Jesus as God's salvation because he has been waiting for it; and he has been waiting precisely because the Holy Spirit has revealed to him that the promise of the prophets will be fulfilled during his lifetime (Luke 2:25-26). Anna, too, has been waiting in the temple, preparing herself "with fasting and prayer night and day" to see God's salvation. And upon seeing the child she begins to sing praise and to proclaim the good news "to all who were looking for the redemption of Jerusalem" (vv. 37-38).

We should not miss the significance of the "consolation" and "redemption" for which Simeon, Anna, and the other faithful are looking. Anna, in particular, has been living in the temple for perhaps as long as sixty years. This would mean that she has been praying eagerly for "the redemption of Jerusalem" from about the time the Romans captured Jerusalem through military conquest (63 BCE). The "consolation" for which she longs is thus not condolences from God: "That's too bad about the military occupation by Roman soldiers and economic exploitation by the tax collectors and official corruption of the nation-temple establishment. But it's all right now, because the good news is that *beyond history in another world* . . ." Such a message of "comfort" in the "afterlife" is the "gospel" of the conquistador that has for centuries "pacified" the peasant peoples of Latin America while dictators crush the weak and oligarchs plunder the poor. Simeon, Anna, and the other faithful who are gathered in the temple and rejoice at the sight of their Savior are awaiting, not the delivery of a sympathy card from heaven, but deliverance from Egypt and Babylon—a new exodus!

The songs of Zechariah, Mary, and Simeon also reveal this distinctive biblical eschatology. These songs are the voiced hope of those living in the present in the light of the ultimate truth of God's sovereignty, the truth that God reigns over all despite the pretensions and ambitions of Pharaoh, Nebuchadnezzar, and Caesar. Those who sing these songs in faith set their hope for freedom from fear, not on the productivity of the economy or the prowess of the military, but entirely on the possibility that the judgment of God upon the powers of domination, the rulers and authorities of this world, may fall *today*. These songs are the overflowing of hearts filled to the full with the expectation that God's kingdom may "break into" our historical reality at any moment and be realized among us in concrete ways. The poetry of these songs conveys a *palpable* sense that God's kingdom is *imminent*—for Zechariah, Mary, and Simeon, the salvation and peace of God is anything but "spiritualized" or "futurized."

Biblical hope is a sharp awareness for the redemptive tension between "today" and "tomorrow"—

> that God's future is *now* impinging upon our historical present
> and declaring the evil age of this fallen world to be passing,
> that God's light is *now* breaking upon our darkness of nationalism and racism
> and declaring the night of exile to be ending,
> that God's freedom is *now* marching into our brickyards and sweatshops
> and declaring the chain of slavery to be breaking,
> that God's justice is *now* overturning the orders of oppression and exploitation
> and declaring the power of domination to be waning,
> that God's peace is *now* overcoming the forces of materialism and militarism
> and declaring the foundation of empire to be crumbling.

Biblical hope—grounded upon the historical revelation of God's kingdom in the life, death, and resurrection of Jesus—is the live anticipation of the imminent fulfillment of God's kingdom of salvation, of freedom and justice and peace. This hope is not waiting for "the end of history." This hope is expectant looking that believes that God's promise of salvation is alive and renewable to every generation in every era of history. This hope is trustful watching that believes that "the darkness of the present age" is lifting, that a new dawn is about to break, revealing a saving act of God that brings near God's kingdom.

The faith of this hope is expressed in the shout, "Maranatha!"—"Our Lord, come!" (1 Cor 16:22).

Amen! Come, Lord Jesus!

NOTES

1. Cited from Plato, *The Republic*, trans. R.E. Allen (New Haven: Yale University Press, 2006), 55–56.

2. Joseph Hart, "Come, Ye Sinners" (1759), cited from http://www.hymnary.org.

3. "Letter from Birmingham Jail" (April 16, 1963).

4. Emphases in Scripture quotations are added.

5. Quoted from "I Will Tear Down My Barns," in *On Social Justice: St. Basil the Great*, trans. C. Paul Schroeder, 59–71 (Crestwood, NY: St. Vladimir's Seminary, 2009).

6. Cited from Rev. C. T. Vivian (sermon on Amos 3:10-11, St. Paul-Bethel Missionary Baptist Church, South Bend, IN, 2003).

7. Excerpted from "Where Do We Go From Here," in *A Testament of Hope: The Essential Writings and Speeches of Martin Luther King, Jr.*, ed. James M. Washington, 245–52 (San Francisco: HarperSanFrancisco, 1986).

8. Cited from Ulrich Mauser, *The Gospel of Peace: A Scriptural Message for Today's World* (Louisville, KY: Westminster/John Knox, 1992), 87–88.

9. For further details of and reflection on Dirk Willems, see Alan Kreider, Eleanor Kreider, and Paulus Widjaja, *A Culture of Peace: God's Vision for the Church* (Intercourse, PA: Good Books, 2005), 52–57.

10. Excerpted from "I See the Promised Land," in *A Testament of Hope*, 279–86.

11. Quoted from *We Shall Not Be Moved*, directed by Bernie Hargis (Worcester, PA: Gateway Films, 2002).

12. Cited from *Voices of the Civil Rights Movement: Black American Freedom Songs 1960–1966* (Washington, DC: Smithsonian Folkways Recordings, 1997).

13. Quoted from "*Playboy* Interview: Martin Luther King, Jr.," in *A Testament of Hope*, 348, original emphasis.

14. Cited from *Amandla! A Revolution in Four-Part Harmony* (New York: ATO Records, 2003).

15. John Behr, trans., *On the Apostolic Preaching: St. Irenaeus of Lyons* (Crestwood, NY: St. Vladimir's Seminary, 1997), sect. 61. See also Kreider, *A Culture of Peace*, 10–11.

16. Excerpted from Christian Wolf, "Seek the Peace of the City—Now More Than Ever," in *The Revolution of the Candles: Christians in the Revolution of the German Democratic Republic*, Jörg Swoboda, 173–84 (Macon, GA: Mercer University Press, 1996).

BIBLIOGRAPHY

While this book is not a strictly scholarly work, it is in much of its substance the fruit of serious study. The list below comprises those works that have most significantly shaped my thinking as reflected in this book.

Anabaptist and Benedictine Tradition

Snyder, C. Arnold. *Following in the Footsteps of Christ: The Anabaptist Tradition*. Maryknoll, NY: Orbis, 2004.

Stewart, Columba, OSB. *Prayer and Community: The Benedictine Tradition*. Maryknoll, NY: Orbis, 1998.

Biblical Interpretation and Imagination

Brown, Robert MacAfee. *Unexpected News: Reading the Bible with Third World Eyes*. Philadelphia: Westminster, 1984.

Brueggemann, Walter. *Israel's Praise: Doxology against Idolatry and Ideology*. Philadelphia: Fortress, 1988.

———. *Finally Comes the Poet: Daring Speech for Proclamation*. Minneapolis: Fortress, 1989.

———. *The Prophetic Imagination*. 2nd ed. Minneapolis: Fortress, 2001.

Johnson, Luke Timothy. *Living Jesus: Learning the Heart of the Gospel*. San Francisco: HarperSanFrancisco, 1999.

Kraybill, Donald B. *The Upside-Down Kingdom*. Rev. ed. Scottdale, PA: Herald, 1990.

Wink, Walter. *Engaging the Powers: Discernment and Resistance in a World of Domination*. Minneapolis: Fortress, 1992.

Wright, N.T. *The Challenge of Jesus: Rediscovering Who Jesus Was and Is*. Downers Grove, IL: InterVarsity, 1999.

Yoder Neufeld, Thomas R. *Ephesians*. Scottdale, PA: Herald, 2002.

The Gospel of Luke

Brown, Raymond E. *The Birth of the Messiah: A Commentary on the Infancy Narratives in the Gospels of Matthew and Luke*. New updated ed. New York: Doubleday, 1993.

Cassidy, Richard J. *Jesus, Politics, and Society: A Study of Luke's Gospel*. Maryknoll, NY: Orbis, 1978.

Evans, Craig A., and James A. Sanders. *Luke and Scripture: The Function of Sacred Tradition in Luke-Acts*. Minneapolis: Fortress, 1993.

Grassi, Joseph. *Peace on Earth: Roots and Practices from Luke's Gospel*. Collegeville, MN: Liturgical Press, 2004.

Horsley, Richard A. *Galilee: History, Politics, People*. Valley Forge, PA: Trinity, 1995.

Johnson, Luke Timothy. *The Gospel of Luke*. Edited by Daniel J. Harrington. Sacra Pagina Series. Collegeville, MN: Liturgical Press, 1991.

Maynard-Reid, Pedrito U. *Complete Evangelism: The Luke-Acts Model*. Scottdale, PA: Herald, 1997.

Swartley, Willard M. *Israel's Scripture Traditions and the Synoptic Gospels: Story Shaping Story*. Peabody, MA: Hendrickson, 1994.

Talbert, Charles A. *Reading Luke: A Literary and Theological Commentary on the Third Gospel*. Macon, GA: Smyth & Helwys, 2002.

Tannehill, Robert C. *The Narrative Unity of Luke-Acts: A Literary Interpretation*. Vol. 1, *The Gospel according to Luke*. Philadelphia: Fortress, 1986. Vol. 2, *The Acts of the Apostles*. Minneapolis: Fortress, 1990.

Salvation, Justice, and Peace

Hauerwas, Stanley. *The Peaceable Kingdom: A Primer in Christian Ethics*. Notre Dame, IN: University of Notre Dame, 1983.

Kreider, Alan. *Journey Towards Holiness: A Way of Living for God's Nation*. Scottdale, PA: Herald, 1987.

Kreider, Alan, Eleanor Kreider, and Paulus Widjaja. *A Culture of Peace: God's Vision for the Church*. Intercourse, PA: Good Books, 2005.

Malchow, Bruce V. *Social Justice in the Hebrew Bible*. Collegeville, MN: Liturgical Press, 1996.

Marshall, Christopher D. *Crowned with Glory and Honor: Human Rights in the Biblical Tradition*. Telford, PA: Pandora, 2001.

Mauser, Ulrich. *The Gospel of Peace: A Scriptural Message for Today's World*. Louisville, KY: Westminster/John Knox, 1992.

Romero, Oscar. *The Violence of Love*. Farmington, PA: Plough, 1998.

Snyder Belousek, Darrin W. *Atonement, Justice, and Peace: The Message of the Cross and the Mission of the Church*. Grand Rapids, MI: Eerdmans, 2012.

Swartley, Willard M. *Covenant of Peace: The Missing Peace in New Testament Theology and Ethics*. Grand Rapids, MI: Eerdmans, 2006.

Yoder, John Howard. *The Original Revolution: Essays on Christian Pacifism*. Scottdale, PA: Herald, 1971.

———. *The Politics of Jesus*. Grand Rapids, MI: Eerdmans, 1972.

———. *For the Nations: Essays Public and Evangelical*. Grand Rapids, MI: Eerdmans, 1997.

Yoder, Perry B. *Shalom: The Bible's Word for Salvation, Justice, and Peace*. Nappanee, IN: Evangel, 1987.

SCRIPTURE INDEX